# ICELAND

## LAND of the SAGAS

### TEXT BY DAVID ROBERTS
### PHOTOGRAPHS BY JON KRAKAUER

VILLARD   NEW YORK

PAGE 1:    Sea stacks guard the coast of Heimaey Island.

PAGE 2–3:    Dusk falls on Stapafell, satellite peak to Snae-fellsjökull. Elves are supposed to dwell in a rock on its summit.

PAGE 4:    The harbor of Heimaey in the Westman Islands remains the most important seaport in Iceland.

PAGE 5:    (Left) A rare hexagonal church with belfry to match serves parishoners at Silfrastaðir in the north. (Right) At Bolungarvik in the Westfjords a mountain wall looms over the church and village.

PAGE 8–9:    A tongue on the glacier Vatnajökull slides past near Skaftafell.

PAGE 10–11:    A lonely shore near Keflavík on the Reykjanes Peninsula in winter: in the background a boat trawls for cod, the fish that has sustained Iceland's economy for eleven centuries.

EDITOR: ROBERT MORTON

DESIGNER: JENNIFER CLARK

TEXT COPYRIGHT ©1990 BY DAVID ROBERTS

PHOTOS COPYRIGHT ©1990 BY JON KRAKAUER

ALL RIGHTS RESERVED UNDER INTERNATIONAL AND PAN-AMERICAN COPYRIGHT CONVENTIONS. PUBLISHED IN THE UNITED STATES BY VILLARD BOOKS, A DIVISION OF RANDOM HOUSE, INC., NEW YORK, AND SIMULTANEOUSLY IN CANADA BY RANDOM HOUSE OF CANADA LIMITED, TORONTO.

THIS EDITION PUBLISHED BY ARRANGEMENT WITH HARRY N. ABRAMS, INCORPORATED.

VILLARD BOOKS IS A REGISTERED TRADEMARK OF RANDOM HOUSE, INC.

LIBRARY OF CONGRESS CATALOGING-IN-PUBLICATION DATA

ROBERTS, DAVID.
    ICELAND: LAND OF THE SAGAS / TEXT BY DAVID ROBERTS; PHOTOGRAPHS BY JON KRAKAUER.
      P.  CM.
    ISBN 0-375-75267-6 (PBK.: ALK. PAPER)
    1. ICELAND—DESCRIPTION AND TRAVEL.   2. SAGAS.
    I. KRAKAUER, JON.  II. TITLE.
    DL315.R64   1998
    949.12—DC21   98-24618

RANDOM HOUSE WEBSITE ADDRESS: WWW.RANDOMHOUSE.COM

PRINTED IN HONG KONG ON ACID-FREE PAPER

9 8 7 6 5 4 3 2

FIRST VILLARD BOOKS EDITION

THE AUTHORS GRATEFULLY ACKNOWLEDGE THE ASSISTANCE OF THE FOLLOWING:

**The North Face**

**Fuji Photo Film Company**

**Icelandair and Bill Connors**

**Geysir Car Rental**

**Helga and Ágúst Valfells**

**Jónas Kristjánsson**

**Polar Hestar Stables**

**Jon Eiríksson**

**Gróa Asgeirsdóttir**

**Húgrun Linda Gudmundsdóttir**
   **(Miss Iceland 1989)**

**Susan Dirk**

**Gary Sutto**

**Jim Balog**

**Max Gartenberg**

# CONTENTS

THE SUN RISES ABOUT 4:00
A.M. IN JULY ON THE SLOPES
OF NÁMAFJALL NEAR MÝVATN.
THE BLACK CINDER CONE OF
HVERFJALL LIES IN THE
MIDDLE DISTANCE.

# OF MONKS
# AND
# VIKINGS

IN THE SECOND HALF OF THE NINTH CENTURY, A VIKING
named Flóki Vilgerðarson set sail westward from Norway in search of
a rumored land in the North Atlantic. His only navigational aid, we are
told, was a trio of ravens. Once released, the first flew back to Norway;
the second circled and landed on the ship; the third guided Flóki straight to
the new land.

Intending to settle, Flóki put livestock out to graze, but he became so
preoccupied with the excellent fishing that he neglected to make hay for his
animals. During the winter all of them died. The disgusted pioneer decided
to return to Norway. Before abandoning his lonely homestead, he climbed a
mountain, from which he saw drift-ice floating in a distant fjord. The sight
gave him an idea. To discourage other would-be settlers, Flóki named the
new country Iceland. A little more than a century later, another Viking, Eirík
the Red, would pull off quite the opposite scam, luring settlers to a vast
wasteland dominated by a featureless icecap by calling his find Greenland.

Flóki's bad news, however, failed to dissuade the bold sailors of Norway,
for word had leaked out that Iceland, far from being a frozen wilderness, was
a mild and lovely place, seamed with salmon-thronged rivers and ringed
with lush green meadows. (A shipmate of Flóki's had reported that in Iceland "every blade of grass was bedewed with butter.")

The first permanent Icelandic settler, Ingólf Arnarson, arrived in 874 A.D.
Vikings were great believers in submitting to a preordained fate. As his ship
lay in sight of land, Ingólf followed the approved practice and threw over-

board his high-seat pillars—ornamented wooden posts that flanked the master's chair in every Norwegian house. Where they drifted to shore, there Ingólf would build. The pillars fetched up near a place on the southwest coast that steamed with hot springs. Ingólf named the spot "Bay of Smoke"—in Old Norse, Reykjavík.

Eleven centuries later, Iceland remains a country surprisingly little known beyond its borders. Americans in particular suffer from ignorance of the place, even though Reykjavík lies closer to New York City than San Francisco does. Only about 30,000 American visitors a year set foot in Iceland, most of them tourists making token layovers on their way to Europe. (For perspective, compare this number to the four and a half million who visit Maine's Acadia National Park each year.)

Since 1944, when it won full autonomy from Denmark, Iceland has been an independent European nation. The island's area is 39,690 square miles—about the size of Virginia, or a little larger than Hungary. Yet Iceland's population is a mere 250,000, the number of inhabitants of a middling city such as Corpus Christi, Texas. Iceland is more sparsely populated by a factor of six than any other European country, Norway being its closest rival.

Yet any notion of the country as a rude, backward former colony is grievously in error. With the founding of a national assembly called the Althing in 930, Iceland invented out of thin air what has often been called Europe's first parliament. Slavery had vanished by 1117. Illiteracy was wiped out in the eighteenth century. Iceland adopted women's suffrage in 1915, five years before the United States. The current president of Iceland, Vigdis Finnbogadóttir, was the first woman anywhere in the world to be elected as a head of state.

---

Pronunciation Guide: To the English speaker's ear, Icelandic sounds like an exotic, subtly inflected tongue. It may also look all but unpronounceable on the page. To read this book, one need know nothing about Icelandic pronunciation. Yet many readers may find it disturbing not to be able to shape proper names in the mind's ear.

What follows is a much oversimplified guide to the sounds of the Icelandic language.

Eth (ð) is pronounced like the voiced *th*, as in "bathe."

Thorn (þ) , pronounced like the unvoiced *th* in "bath," has been rendered throughout this text as *th*, in keeping with standard English practice.

One will not, on the whole, go far wrong pronouncing five vowels with their full, open European sounds: e.g. *a* as in "father," *e* as in "grey," *i* as in "piano," *o* as in "so," *u* as in "assume." However:

*á* = "ow" as in "town"

*ae* = "i" as in "high"

*au* is like the French "eui" as in "feuille"

*ö* is like the German "ö" as in "möglich"

Most of the consonants sound roughly as they do in English. But

*j* = "y" as in "yes"

*g* is always hard as in "give"

*r* is trilled

Some of the strangest Icelandic sounds are paired consonants. Thus

*ll* = something like "tl" as in "settle"

*nn* = something like "tn" as in an abbreviated "fatten"

*fn* = something like "pn" as in an abbreviated "happen"

*fl* = something like "pl" as in "couple"

*hv* = "qu" as in "question"

Stress in Icelandic is relatively regular, almost always falling on the first syllable.

ON A WINTER AFTERNOON, A NATURAL HOT SPRING INSIDE THE CITY LIMITS OF REYKJAVÍK OFFERS A PLEASANT DIVERSION.

OVERLEAF: CLASSIC VICTORIAN HOUSES, WITH WALLS OF CORRUGATED IRON, LINE THE WEST SHORE OF THE TJÖRNIN.

With a population of 90,000, Reykjavík has today the sophistication of a European capital. The city teems with poets, chess experts, performance artists, and avant-garde sculptors. There are posh restaurants serving nouvelle cuisine and boutiques flaunting Parisian and Milanese fashions. In its forward-looking urbanity, Reykjavík became one of the first cities in the world to ban dogs—despite an age-old reverence for the purebred Icelandic sheepdog. In Iceland twenty times as many books are published per capita as in the United States. The country has one of the highest per capita incomes in the world, and a life expectancy (73.9 years for men, 80.2 for women) matched only by Japan's.

The whole of Iceland lies within four degrees of the Arctic Circle. Yet the Gulf Stream warms its shores and ameliorates its climate: New York City is colder in winter than Reykjavík is. By and large, the country is unforested: the only indigenous trees are dwarf birches, which cling in scraggly stands to anomalous pockets of warmth. The bareness of the countryside gives woods-loving visitors the willies. Others consider Iceland one of the most beautiful places in the world. Especially in midsummer, when it grows as dark as dusk for only a few hours around midnight, the slanting play of sun conjures up, in the poet A. E. Housman's phrase, a land of lost content. Another poet, W. H. Auden, who came to Iceland on a lark in 1936, revisited the country almost three decades afterwards. "In my childhood dreams," he later wrote, "Iceland was holy ground; when, at the age of twenty-nine, I saw it for the first time, the reality verified my dream; at fifty-seven it was holy ground still, with the most magical light of anywhere on earth."

LEFT: THE BLUE LAGOON, A BIZARRE SPA IN THE MIDDLE OF A LAVA WASTELAND TO THE SOUTH OF REYKJAVÍK, IS NOT A HOT SPRING BUT A LAKE HEATED BY THE POWER PLANT VISIBLE IN THE BACKGROUND. A WHITE MUD THAT COATS THE FLOOR OF THE LAKE, CONSIDERED A CURE FOR PSORIASIS, IS SOLD BY THE JARFUL IN REYKJAVÍK.

CENTER: REYKJAVÍK, ICELAND'S CAPITAL, LIES BENEATH THE HIGH PLATEAU OF THE ESJA. HERE, THE LEGENDARY FIRST SETTLER'S HIGH-SEAT PILLARS FLOATED ASHORE.

RIGHT: AT HÖFÐI, IN REYKJAVÍK, THE REAGAN-GORBACHEV SUMMIT MEETING WAS HELD IN 1988.

Nature has wrought extravagant wonders upon the Icelandic landscape. It is the most volcanic place in the world: scientists estimate that one-third of all the lava that has burst to the earth's surface in the last 500 years has done so on this island. Residents count on a new eruption every five years or so. Hot springs, steam vents, mud pots, hillsides breathing vapor—the sort of prodigies that make Yellowstone famous world over—are old hat in Iceland. Geysir, whose name has become generic for all waterspouts, lies fifty miles east of Reykjavík. The splendor and variety of Iceland's waterfalls are legion. Although most of the country is ice-free, the sprawling icecap called the Vatnajökull is the largest glacier in Europe.

For a relatively small country that has been explored and traversed for more than a millennium, Iceland remains remarkably wild. Although its highest elevation is only 6,950 feet, the landscape enfolds a number of still-unclimbed mountains. In general, all the towns, villages, and farms in Iceland are found on or near the coast. The central interior is virtually uninhabited. To probe far inland today, even behind the wheel of a Land Rover, is still an adventure. A bulletin of the government tourist board called "Practical Information for Tourists" contains, under the heading "Basic Statistics," this dour self-appraisal of the land:

| | | | |
|---|---|---|---|
| Cultivated | 1% | Glaciers | 12% |
| Grazings | 20% | Sands | 4% |
| Lakes | 3% | Other wasteland | 52% |
| Lavas | 11% | | |

In a place such as southern California, much of what Iceland calls "other wasteland" would be chock-a-block with condominiums. But the tourist board accurately reflects an ancient nordic pragmatism—that only valleys with thick meadows and deep soil are properly habitable.

Today's Icelander prides himself on being au courant with world affairs. He is also likely to be a fervent champion of Icelandic achievements, which range from hosting the Reagan-Gorbachev summit and the Fischer-Spassky chess match to international triumphs in weightlifting competitions, team handball, and beauty contests. In a sense, Icelanders have a weakness for everything trendy, gimmicky, and—yes—American.

Yet deep in the soul of every Icelander, informed by a passion matched by few other peoples in the world (the Greeks come to mind), lurks a fierce attachment to an ancient glory, a putative golden age that ended more than seven hundred years ago. Mention the date 1262 to an Icelander and watch him wince. It was in that year that the nation, crippled by bloody feuds among the six power-crazy clans that had taken control of the land, agreed to submit to the Norwegian crown after nearly four centuries of sovereignty. What followed was even worse, as first Norwegian and then Danish rulers treated their North Atlantic colony with the kind of malign neglect England long lavished on Ireland. Natural disasters—volcanic and epidemic—added to the misery. In 1100, scholars estimate, the population of Iceland was about 70,000. At its low ebb, in 1708, that number was reduced to 34,000.

The inescapable metaphor crops up again and again: for the Icelander looking back on his history, the years from 1262 to the twentieth century—some would say all the way to 1944—were the country's Dark Ages. The epoch before, from Ingólf's landing to 1262, gleams with a burnish reciprocally intense. Nor do those four pioneer centuries blur into a vague, sentimental icon, such as the American notion of our Founding Fathers. The Icelander has a quite specific grasp of what happened in the year 1000.

There are good reasons for this acuteness. Old Norse, which was once the common language of all Scandinavia, has branched and modulated radically in Norway, Sweden, and Denmark, as these nations asserted their identities. Icelandic alone remains close to Old Norse—so close that schoolchildren can read medieval classics with ease. It is as if an American twelve-year-old could put down the Hardy Boys and pick up *Beowulf*.

Around the year 1100, Icelanders began to write in their own language. The next two centuries saw an all but unfathomable flowering of poetry and prose. As Homer built upon a long oral tradition of storytelling and verse, so did the first Icelandic chroniclers and bards. This body of writing is large and complex, but its crowning accomplishment is the prose narratives called the sagas—a collection of works that can lay fair claim to being the pinnacle of medieval European literature.

Most of the sagas* were written in the thirteenth century. All have come

---

*By the sagas, we mean only what are more narrowly called the Sagas of Icelanders. These comprise all the most famous works casually alluded to as "the sagas." In addition, medieval Icelandic authors wrote sagas about the kings of Norway; contemporary sagas about Catholic bishops and leading thirteenth-century families; sagas of chivalry aimed to entertain the Norwegian court; and heroic sagas that retell ancient Scandinavian stories from before the settlement of Iceland.

THE WATERSPOUT CALLED STROKKUR ERUPTS AS HIGH AS 100 FEET EVERY FIVE MINUTES OR SO. IT LIES A FEW YARDS FROM AN ANCIENT WONDER, THE EPONYMOUS GEYSIR, WHICH NOW ERUPTS ONLY AFTER BEING PRIMED WITH SOAP FLAKES.

down to us anonymous; we can guess at the authorship of only one or two. The sagas concentrate on heroes and events that occupied the period from 930 to 1030—called, as one might expect, the Saga Age. During this stirring century, after sixty years devoted to settling Iceland, the Vikings devised an indigenous culture. The central question about the sagas—as knotty today as when it was first critically formulated in the eighteenth century—is to what extent these narratives are history, to what extent fiction. We know that many of the saga heroes such as Guðrún Ósvífrsdóttir and Snorri Goði really existed. In the town of Borgarnes today you can visit Skallagrim Kveldúlfsson's grave. But what can we make of the scene in which Grettir the Strong dives beneath a waterfall to wrestle a she-troll to the death?

For all its wildness, the Icelandic countryside is thick with place names. Most of these are of ancient origin, and a good portion date from the Age of Settlement (874-930) or from the Saga Age. Like few other countries in the world (Greece being one), Iceland has its history and mythology woven into the very landscape. In Greece this embroidery is bodied forth in vivid marble ruins. Because its early settlers built in turf and wood rather than stone Iceland is bare of ruins. The oldest surviving house dates only from 1736.

For the traveler today, a pilgrimage through the country in search of saga sites is thus an exercise both elusive and eloquent. That meadow jutting toward the sea on the west coast may look empty and blank, but we know that Unn the Deep-Minded lost her comb there, probably in the year 916, whence the place ever since has been called Kambsnes. If you walk up to the man mowing his field at Bjarg, a nondescript farmstead in the north, and ask him where Grettir's Lift is, he will guide you to the huge boulder which that hero moved as a test of strength some 980 years ago.

The medieval world that the sagas celebrate amounts for the present-day Icelander to something more basic than a heritage. It is a life-force imminent in his very identity. But for the nightmare of history, he might say, Iceland's glory would still rule the North Atlantic. That instinct of destiny finds its expression in the most quotidian of acts and attitudes. "In a drunken state," writes the poet Sigurður Magnússon of his compatriots, "they *are* Vikings." The World Strongman champion for 1988, Hjalti "Ursus" Árnason, brags, "We power weightlifters are the true Icelanders. What would the Vikings and saga heroes say if they came back here today and found everyone playing chess and handball?"

It is safe to say that without a certain appreciation of the Saga Age, the foreigner cannot really fathom Icelandic character. Nor can he gaze beneath the surface of the storied landscape of this fortunate isle, until he knows something of Burnt Njál and Gísli the Outlaw, of Killer-Hrapp and Ólaf the Peacock, of Hallgerd's refusal to twine her hair and of Glám's dying curse upon Grettir the Strong.

It is extraordinary how quickly and successfully the Vikings settled Iceland after they had discovered it. Before the invention of the compass, simply finding the island on any given voyage was no mean feat. Yet the laconic sailing directions Norwegian captains handed down bear witness to how readily these master mariners turned the 700-mile journey into a milk run.

Not all the voyages went smoothly. No European ships had ever before sailed so far from sight of land. The chief navigational tool was not ravens such as the ones Flóki launched, but plain dead reckoning. A passage from the *Laxdaela Saga* reveals how vital the sense of orientation in a good navigator could be. On a voyage from Norway to Ireland, Ólaf the Peacock's ship drifts becalmed in dense fog. Orn is his pilot.

> At last the fog lifted and the wind began to blow, so they hoisted sail. But now an argument arose about the direction in which Ireland lay, and they could not agree on it. Orn maintained one thing, but most of the others contradicted him and said he was utterly confused, and that the majority should decide. The question was finally referred to Ólaf, and Ólaf said, "I want only the shrewdest to decide; in my opinion the counsel of fools is all the more dangerous the more of them there are."

Orn guides the ship, of course, straight to Ireland.

By the ninth century, the Vikings had become the finest sailors in Europe, and probably in the world. Their *hafskip* had a side rudder and a single square sail. It was a large ship, weighing perhaps forty tons, capable of carrying forty men, livestock, food, and furniture and building timbers for the settlers.

With this incomparable vessel, and the art of hand-to-hand combat honed in generations of home-grown feuds, the Vikings soon became the most feared warriors in Europe. From what is now Norway, Denmark, and Sweden, these merciless raiders pillaged west, south, and east. They forged down the great Russian rivers all the way to the Black and Caspian seas. In Constantinople, Viking mercenaries formed the Varangians, an elite palace guard for the Byzantine emperor. Vikings conquered large parts of Britain, and sailed up the Seine to lay siege to Paris. (A frequent prayer in the churches of northern France was, "From the wrath of the Northmen, O Lord, deliver us.") Vikings circled Spain to enter the Mediterranean, where they battered Arab strongholds. Norse explorers discovered Greenland in 982 (it may have been sighted some eighty years earlier) and North America four years later.

Many passages in the sagas describe Viking raids. Although the authors of these thirteenth-century works had become Christians, there is no room in their accounts for pity or remorse. Nor do they waste any breath justifying these gratuitous attacks on moral grounds. They take the pre-Christian view: pillaging and murdering in foreign lands were simply what a Viking did. Thus the author of *Egil's Saga* blandly appraises the raids of a young Norwegian named Thórólf and his cronies:

> There was plenty of loot, so each of them had a good share. That's how things stood for a number of years: every summer they'd go out on viking expeditions and then spend winter at home with their fathers. Thórólf brought his parents back a lot of valuable things. In those days there was ample opportunity for a man to grow rich and famous.

The immediate cause of Iceland's settlement was the tyranny of King Harald Finehair, who in 872 became the first monarch to unify Norway's scattered chiefdoms into something like a state. When Harald demanded of other lords either submission or exile, many chose to try their luck in the newly reported land to the west.

Although the course of Icelandic history was set once and for all by the Viking settlement, Norwegians were not the first people to discover the island. When the first Norse sailors arrived, they found a few small bands of men already in residence. These were Irish monks who had fled their homeland the better to worship God in an austere setting. As astounding as the Viking nautical achievement is, it is matched by the pluck and skill of these hermits who, before the end of the eighth century, crossed more than 500 miles of open sea in their flimsy *currachs*, or skin boats, then scratched a living from fish, weeds, and faith on the shore of an unknown land.

The coexistence of Vikings and monks was short-lived. Unwilling to share their wilderness with pagans, the Irish fled—some think to Greenland, though there is no firsthand evidence for this. We know almost nothing about these brave *papar*, as the Norsemen called the monks. Their very existence in Iceland might be considered apocryphal, but for the fact that the earliest Icelandic histories from the twelfth century mention them, quite independently of the corroborative ninth-century account of Dicuil, an Irish geographer living in France. There are a few Irish place names on the coast of Iceland that hint at eighth-century monastic retreats, several of which are associated with all-but-vanished stone walls that authorities deem Irish.

It may seem odd, given the natural fertility of Iceland, that no early aboriginal migrations found their way to the island. Thanks to the Irish and Norse priority, Iceland is the only land in the world without a prehistory; i.e., the only land whose first human inhabitants were literate. For the Vikings, once the strange hermits were cleared out of the way, this meant that they beheld a country in which the land was free for the taking, with no need to subdue natives or to build in defensive clusters such as those formed by most medieval European towns. The pattern of settlement, which is quite evenly spread around Iceland's perimeter, was set in the first sixty years.

There were, in fact, no towns at all in ninth- or tenth-century Iceland: only farmsteads. Despite the twentieth-century boom of Reykjavík and the country's surge into modernity, the ancient pattern holds strong today. In the whole of Iceland, there are only sixty towns and villages, while there are 4,500 farms. The stability of the latter figure is remarkable: one scholar estimates that in the year 1100, there were 4,560 farms in Iceland. As you drive across the countryside, you will see many a modern farmhouse, but the odds are that the name of the place goes back eight or nine centuries.

During the long pall of Iceland's Dark Ages after 1262, there was virtually no immigration; indeed, there is virtually none today. The consequence is that the ethnic makeup of the population has remained exceptionally stable for a millennium. On their way to Iceland from Norway, Vikings customarily stopped in Ireland to capture slaves. The only significant admixture in what would otherwise be a "pure" Nordic strain is thus the Irish contribution. (Even today, for an Icelander to have red hair carries the faint stigma that he or she is the descendant of slaves.)

One of the unsolved anthropological questions about Iceland is the relative weight of Irish and Norwegian blood in the population. There is scarcely a single Gaelic loan-word in modern Icelandic, but this is not surprising, given the power discrepancy between masters and slaves. The proportion of early Irish settlers has often been set around ten to fifteen percent, but recent studies of blood-group distribution suggest a much higher percentage. Over the years, scholars have argued vehemently about the Irish impact on the nation's culture. A Reykjavík wag sums up the debate thus: "You must remember that we are a cross between the most boring people in the world and the drunkenest."

AMONG THE STRANGEST PLACES IN ICELAND ARE ITS LAVA TUBES, VOLCANIC CAVES FORMED BY HEATED GASES. IN SAGA TIMES, OUTLAWS SOMETIMES HID IN THESE CAVES, YET NOT ALL OF THEM HAVE BEEN DISCOVERED OR FULLY EXPLORED. HERE, IN THE RAUFARHÓLSHELLIR, EVEN IN SUMMER THE FLOOR IS FESTOONED WITH STALAGMITE-LIKE PILLARS OF ICE.

OVERLEAF: AT 9:00 P.M., THE LAST SUNLIGHT OF A JULY DAY STRIKES A FARMSTEAD BESIDE THE THJÓRSÁ RIVER IN THE SOUTHWEST.

In the absence of any government, power in the new country tended to be vested in men who had large holdings of land, livestock, and slaves. They enlisted less-affluent neighbors as followers, and consolidated their sway with carefully arranged marriages. It was inevitable that these men, who were in effect local chieftains, would come into conflict with one another over such issues as land claims, grazing rights, and ownership of driftwood. Men who had grown rich pillaging and raiding were not likely to sit down and reason things out, and many a murderous outcome sprang from a petty quarrel. Within half a century of Ingólf's landing, the need for law had made itself obvious.

According to Iceland's first historian, a wise man name Úlfljót was chosen to go to Norway, study the legal code that obtained there, and recommend a body of law for Iceland. Meanwhile his foster-brother, Grím, was asked to reconnoiter the country and select a permanent spot for an assembly.

In 930 the first Althing was convened. Grím had chosen a broad valley just north of the Thingvallavatn, Iceland's largest lake. Thingvellir, as the assembly place is called, has become Iceland's most hallowed location. When the 1,100th anniversary of the Althing was celebrated in 1974, 50,000 Icelanders attended—almost one-quarter of the country's population.

Grím's choice was inspired. Thingvellir, which lies thirty miles east of Reykjavík, has one of the most striking settings in Iceland. A sharp volcanic rift tears longitudinally through the gentle valley, creating a cliff about 150 feet high. The lovely Öxará River plunges off the cliff in a waterfall, winds beneath

LEFT: A BASALT OUTCROP CROWNS AN UNNAMED HILL NEAR THE SOUTHWESTERN SEAPORT OF THORLÁKSHÖFN.

RIGHT: THINGVELLIR, WHERE ICELAND BECAME A NATION IN 930 A.D., LIES BELOW THE IGNEOUS CLIFF CALLED THE ALMANNAGJÁ. ACROSS THE ÖXARÁ RIVER STANDS A VICTORIAN CHURCH ON THE SITE WHERE ICELAND'S FIRST CHURCH WAS BUILT IN 1018.

the precipice, and empties into the vast lake. To the northeast on a clear day you can see the Langjökull, one of Iceland's largest icecaps. On a low ridge beneath the cliff, the various clans that came from all over Iceland built their booths—unroofed stone-walled rectangles which they would cover with tenting each summer. Sheltered by the vertical rift, yet open to the valley, these booths were delightfully placed: the whole scene reawakens in today's visitor the childhood urge to play house in the outdoors. The grassed-over lumps and ridges of some of the booths (mostly from the seventeenth and eighteenth centuries) can still be seen.

Thirty-six of the most powerful chieftains became *goðar* (singular *goði*), with duties that ranged from serving in the Althing to taking charge of religious observances in their home districts. (The word *goði*, which is related to "god," is sometimes translated as "priest-chieftain.") The Althing was held for two weeks every June. Each *goði* was obliged to attend, and his prestige was enhanced by the number of followers he could bring with him to share his booth. For those living in the northeast of Iceland, this meant an annual journey of 300 or 400 miles. Among their other accomplishments, the Viking settlers were superb equestrians, who undertook long treks on horseback, fording dangerous rivers, even in winter, without a second thought.

The Althing had a profound social function. Booths vied with one another in holding grand feasts and handing out valuable gifts. A year's worth of gossip and news was eagerly traded from one parish to another. Often the assembly resembled a long drunk. But by meeting annually and agreeing to

OVERLEAF: REMNANTS OF ICELAND'S ARCHITECTURAL PAST, A TRIO OF SOD-ROOFED HOUSES ARE ALL THAT REMAINS OF THE ABANDONED FISHING VILLAGE OF HVALNES.

submit to law, the scattered chieftaincies began to cohere in a nation.

From among the *goðar*, one man was elected Law Speaker, the most important post in Iceland. He served a three-year term. Each summer, it was his duty to stand on the Law Rock and recite from memory (for Iceland as yet had no written texts) one-third of the law code. If he forgot some statute, and no one corrected him, that law became obsolete—an admirable practice that modern legislatures might do well to emulate.

Some of the laws strike us today as colorfully quaint. There were dozens of regulations pertaining to horses, including the following: "If a man climbs on the back of a man's horse without permission, he incurs a fine of six ounces. Now if he rides away, then he incurs a payment of three marks." A woman was allowed to own land, but the limit of her holdings was set at the size of the territory she could walk around, leading a two-year-old heifer, from dawn to sunset on a spring day.

The crucial purpose of the Althing was to settle disputes peacefully. Before 930, a man wronged had no recourse but to take revenge on his oppressor. Now he had an alternative: to bring his suit before the national assembly. Each of the four quadrants of Iceland had its own court at the Althing, where such disputes were adjudicated (a fifth court was later added). Even a just killing, such as one in self-defense, required compensation, and out of the judgments rendered at the Althing Iceland developed its first monetary system. Its standard was ounces of gold or silver, but the everyday unit became the ell, a measured quantity of homespun woolen cloth.

All too often it happened that the contending parties could not reach an agreement. In such a case, the two chief foes waded out to an island in the Öxará and came to terms with sword and halberd. (The Icelandic word for "duel," *hólmganga*, means literally "island-going.")

The Althing was a dazzling innovation in history. If it was not quite, in the modern sense, a parliament, it was still an extraordinary experiment in democracy at a time when every other country in Europe was resolutely feudal and monarchical. But the great weakness of Iceland's government was that, while it boasted a legislature and a judiciary, it had no executive branch. (Contemporary historians elsewhere in Europe recorded in shocked tones that Iceland was a country without a king.) A judgment rendered at the Althing did not automatically take effect: it was up to the party who brought the suit to enforce it.

Because of this problem, the deliberations of the Althing were frequently in vain. Sometimes the process broke down in midstream, and more than one pitched battle was fought on the spot, among the booths at Thingvellir. More often the disagreeing parties took their grievances back home with them, where they surfaced eventually in blood. For the Viking settlers were proud and aggressive folk, with long memories for insult and injury. The sagas reflect this fact: their central, repetitive theme is feud and retribution, depredation and revenge. One scholar has calculated that in the forty-odd sagas that have come down to us, there are 520 instances of feud, only ten percent of which were settled legally.

Thingvellir today is a national park, one of only three in Iceland. Although in summer several buses daily deposit tourists there, the place is surprisingly unspoiled, with an innocuous modern hotel the only distraction from the past. You can climb a path and hike along the cliff edge, from which vantage the faint outlines of the old booths are best visible, and the lake stretches gloriously to the south. Or you can saunter along the Öxará, pausing beside a serene, still basin with a macabre history: this is the Drowning Pool, where in the sixteenth century women adulterers and heretics were put to death (men were beheaded). After two centuries of scholarly haggling over exactly where the Law Rock was, the government has raised a tall flagpole on a mound amid the ancient booths to proclaim its conjecture.

An exquisite little church, dating from 1859, stands on the very site where the first church in Iceland was built in 1018. Before it lies the boulder on which, according to tradition, the ells of cloth were measured out a thousand years ago. A deep cleft in the earth north of the church, through which a branch of the Öxará flows, is the site of Flosi's Leap. During a free-for-all that broke out at the Althing around 1012, the saga hero Flosi Thórðarsson supposedly escaped from his pursuers by vaulting this chasm. It looks today like a good twenty-foot jump, no paltry deed for a man wearing metal armor and carrying his weapons.

Flosi appears in Njál's Saga, the longest of the sagas and, in the view of many, the finest. The English critic W. P. Ker called it "one of the great prose works of the world." The loose, episodic sweep of the narrative coheres around the doings of two best friends, Gunnar Hámundarson and Njál Thórgeirsson, who in very different ways exemplify the medieval Icelandic ideal of the hero. As it spans nearly a century of history, the tale richly delineates Iceland during the Saga Age; it contains, among other things, the best account in any saga of the adoption of Christianity in the year 1000.

Njál's Saga is also the only saga set in the south of Iceland. Mariners knew the south shore to be a graveyard for ships—"nothing but sands and vast deserts and a harborless coast, and, outside the skerries, a heavy surf." Most of the voyages of settlement skirted this coast well to the south, rounded the southwest corner of Iceland, and, aided by the Gulf Stream, glided into the generous harbors of the west. The south coast was the last in Iceland to be settled. Even today, along a stretch of 220 miles of coastline, there is only the single harbor town of Vík.

The climactic event in Njál's Saga is the Burning, when Njál's enemies trap him with his family in his own house and set fire to it. This vividly rendered scene is probably the single most famous incident in the sagas. For every Icelander, the Burning has a resonance that is hard for an American to fathom: Washington and his cherry tree cast a pale shadow in comparison.

The farmstead where Njál was burned is called Bergthórshvoll. It stands on a low hill in marshland less than two miles from the sea. In the United States, a site of such importance would be a national monument; in France or Germany, it would be surrounded by souvenir stands. In Iceland, as you meander along the narrow dirt roads that lead to Bergthórshvoll, not so much as a single sign announces the proximity of a sacred place. At the site itself, there is only a neatly lettered blue-and-yellow sign naming the farmstead, the same indicator that marks every other farmhouse in the country.

Viewed through morning sea-fog on a summer's day, with the grass before it soaked with dew, the ramshackle farmhouse that stands today at Bergthórshvoll, dating perhaps from the 1940s, looks bucolic, an image out of Wyeth. Early in the twelfth century a compendium called Landnámabók, or Book of Settlements, was composed. This remarkable work lists the

OVERLEAF: DURING THE SAGA AGE, FLOSI, WHO HAD LED THE FORCES THAT BURNED NJÁL'S FAMILY TO DEATH IN THEIR OWN FARMSTEAD, SUPPOSEDLY LEAPT ACROSS THIS CHASM AT THINGVELLIR WITH HIS ARMOR ON TO ESCAPE HIS PURSUERS.

genealogies of some 430 of Iceland's early settlers. Among them is one Njáll, who, says *Landnámabók*, was burned in his house at Bergthórshvoll with six or seven other people; other annals give us the approximate date of 1010. An excavation at the farmstead has demonstrated that a house was burned there sometime during the first two centuries of settlement.

Thus Njál really existed and was probably burned to death with his family early in the eleventh century. As you stand in the fog gazing at the house on the knoll today, with the anonymous saga-author's complex portrait of Njál in mind, you face the classic conundrum posed by all ancient literature that weaves together legend, history, and individual fancy.

Njál, says our author, was essentially a man of peace. He had the gift of second sight, and accurately foresaw his own death. In a famous aphorism defending the Althing, Njál predicts, "With laws shall our land be built up but with lawlessness laid waste." His wisdom and honesty hover above the narrative, an implied alternative to the endless bloodletting that otherwise seems to drive the world. At the Burning, he submits to fate with a stoic resignation whose wellsprings are both Christian and pagan. As the flames leap about them, Njál and his wife climb into their bed to die, in a scene as eerie as it is moving.

Gunnar, Njál's best friend and also murdered by treachery, is the man of action rather than contemplation, the greatest fighter of his time, yet a man who more than once avoids a fatal brawl out of a reluctance to kill. Trapped by legal technicalities, Gunnar is outlawed and ordered to leave the country on pain of death. As he rides south toward the coast from his beloved farm at Hliðarendi, his horse stumbles and he looks back. "How lovely the slopes are," he says, "more lovely than they have ever seemed to me before, golden cornfields and new-mown hay. I am going back home, and I will not go away." (These lines, too, are canonical in the heart of every Icelander.) By returning to Hliðarendi, Gunnar ensures, in the doom-ruled universe of the sagas, his death.

Like Njál, Gunnar is ambushed in his house, with only his wife and mother for allies. So great a warrior is he, however, that singlehandedly he holds off his attackers, killing two and wounding sixteen until his bowstring breaks. In desperation he turns to his proud wife Hallgerd and says, "Let me have two locks of your hair, and help my mother plait them into a bow-string for me." "Does anything depend on it?" asks Hallgerd coolly. "My life depends on it," answers Gunnar, "for they will never overcome me as long as I can use my bow." But Hallgerd remembers a time years before when Gunnar had slapped her face, and she refuses. "To each his own way of earning fame," says Gunnar. "You shall not be asked again." He fights until exhaustion and his wounds overcome him. "The killing of Gunnar," says the saga, "was condemned throughout the land, and many people mourned him deeply."

The *Landnámabók* and other early sources record Gunnar and some of his battles. He, too, was unmistakably a real person. The farmstead of Hliðarendi, too lovely for Gunnar to leave, lies on another back road, scarcely a dozen miles as the crow flies from Bergthórshvoll. No more fuss is made today of this hallowed site than of Njál's. According to the saga, Gunnar lies buried on the hill above the farm—or rather, sits buried, for it was the Norse fashion to inter a dead warrior in the upright position, as if he might still look out upon the world, demanding vengeance from the grave.

ICELAND'S LONGEST RIVER, THE HVITÁ, THUNDERS THROUGH A DEEP GORGE OF SHALE AT GULLFOSS, ONE OF THE COUNTRY'S MOST MAJESTIC WATERFALLS.

OVERLEAF: THE PRESENT-DAY FARMSTEAD AT BERGTHÓRSHVOLL, WHERE NJÁL AND HIS FAMILY WERE BURNED TO DEATH BY HIS ENEMIES AROUND 1011: NO SITE HAS A GREATER MYTHIC RESONANCE FOR THE ICELANDER.

A WINDSWEPT TABLELAND AT
STORHOFÐI PROVIDES GOOD
GRAZING FOR SHEEP ON THE
ISLAND OF HEIMAEY.

# OF HORSES
# AND
# PUFFINS

**A**LITTLE TO THE EAST OF HLIÐARENDI LIES THÓRSMÖRK. Mentioned in *Njál's Saga*, it was in ancient times a natural sanctuary in the wilderness, where men might hide from their pursuers. To the Icelander, Thórsmörk conjures up sylvan enchantment, a flitting, half-magical world like Shakespeare's Arden Forest. An island of tundra just north of the Eyjafjalla icecap, it lies between two braided, silt-bearing rivers, the Markar and the Krossa. Despite these stern surroundings, Thórsmörk, festooned with caves, is a nook of lushness, dense with willows and with birches up to 25 feet tall. In search of shelter, sheep have flocked to this refuge for centuries.

It has never been an easy place to get to. In 1897 the excellent English traveler W. G. Collingwood rode all over Iceland on horseback in quest of saga sites. While he stopped to make gloomy sketches from the gravel bar of the Markar, Collingwood sent his companion, Jón Stefánsson, off with a local guide to investigate Thórsmörk. Stefánsson returned a day later with a rapturous report:

> We spent the night in a cave whose roof and walls were covered with beautiful, tiny ferns, with solitary mountain flowers here and there. The floor was made of soft moss, and the mouth of the cave was closed with thick branches. A streamlet flowing down from the face of an abrupt rock near by lulled us to sleep. It was a warm summer night, and the overhanging glacier gave out a pleasant coolness. Now and then one could hear a sheep bouncing past, to seek new pastures. The murmurs of the glacier, Eyjafjallajökul, under which a volcano sleeps, had a

41

strange sound in the deep silence....

In the morning we explored the rest of the hollows. Their formation, their luxuriant vegetation, little waterfalls, peaks and winding crannies create endless surprises.

You cannot drive a conventional car to Thórsmörk. The best option is to leave your vehicle on the main highway and take a bus, of which there are several each day in midsummer. Like many Icelandic glacial streams, the upper Markar River, which has never been bridged, shifts its channels constantly and so defeats local wisdom about fording places. Stefánsson's guide told him that the river had to be crossed in a different spot every day. On the modern road to Thórsmörk, there are numerous fords; only the high clearance and great weight of a bus are equal to the task, and even so, it makes for a jittery ride.

The mossy caves (carved with names dating back to the eighteenth century) and the winding crannies that Stefánsson found are still there, but the deep silence is gone. For Thórsmörk has become one of the most popular outings in Iceland. Every weekend scores of families camp out under the gnarled birches, but the place belongs to teenagers. On any given Saturday afternoon in July or August, a fair percentage of Reykjavík's fifteen-year-olds can be found in Thórsmörk. They come to hike, to camp, to giggle and gossip and shout, but mostly to drink. For an American, it is a bizarre experience to share a backcountry trail with dozens of staggering teens toting beer cans and vodka-spiked quarts of soda, swilling as they hike.

Bizarre and, at first, dismaying. Teenage drinking, you learn on your first weekend in Reykjavík, is one of Iceland's most troubling problems: if you

LEFT: IN EARLY TIMES THE ICELANDIC SHEEPDOG, AS PURE A STRAIN AS THE ICELANDIC HORSE, WOULD SIT ATOP THE TURF ROOF OF A HOMESTEAD AND GUARD IT AGAINST INTRUDERS.

RIGHT: THÓRSMORK'S LUSH MEADOWS ARE DOTTED WITH DWARF BIRCHES.

walk the streets at 2:00 A.M., you must sidestep thirteen-year-old girls passed out on the sidewalk, fourteen-year-old boys vomiting on the stoops. Yet the scene among the birches at Thórsmörk has a lunatic verve about it: it is not so far in spirit from the intoxications of a Shakespearean forest. And where in America would you find drunkards who love to hike?

There is a long Icelandic tradition of drinking to excess, which the sagas unapologetically celebrate. The exemplar is Egil Skallagrímsson, the hot-tempered hero of *Egil's Saga*. As his English translators comment, Egil is "killer, drunkard, miser, poet, wanderer, farmer." Having outfought his comrades on the field of battle, Egil regularly drinks them under the table in the ale hall. In one of the most grotesque scenes in the saga, after a winter journey floundering through deep snow, Egil and his men come to a farmhouse where they are treated by their host Armod to a perverse hospitality. First, having promised a feast, Armod serves only bowls of curds; then he forces toast after toast of strong ale on the exhausted travelers.

> The drinking was meant to go ahead at full speed, and for a long time Egil kept at it without cheating. When his companions had drunk all they could take, Egil tossed back whatever they couldn't manage....
>
> One man was given the job of serving each toast to Egil and his men, and kept egging them on to drink up quickly, but Egil told his men not to have any more, and he drank their share, that being the only way out of it. When Egil realized that he couldn't keep going any longer, he stood up, walked across the floor to Armod, put both hands on his shoulders and pressed him up against the pillar, then heaved up a vomit of massive proportions that gushed all over Armod's face, into his eyes, nostrils and mouth, and flooded down his chest so that he was almost suffocated.

This salvo threatens to cause a riot, but instead everyone passes out. At dawn, still furious, Egil finds Armod in bed. He seizes his host by the beard and flings an improvised verse of contempt at the hapless fellow. "Then Egil cut off his beard close to the chin, and gouged out an eye with his finger so that it hung out over his cheek. After that Egil went back to his companions and they went their way."

Such passages help account for the behavior of the modern Icelandic man when he is drunk. Normally reticent, well-mannered, and shy, he can become boorishly aggressive, even violent, when the fit is on him. For decades, one of the leading brands of Icelandic beer has been called Egil's Pilsener.

As you travel east from Njál's country, the great icecaps of the Eyjafjalla-jökull and Mýrdalsjökull force you down to the coast. Here is some of the most spectacular country in Iceland, browed by dark igneous cliffs over which waterfalls such as Seljalandsfoss and Skógafoss pour in sudden streams. Just as the south coast was always the most dangerous for sailors, so was it for early travelers on land. Njál's Saga reflects the dread felt by those who had to cross the glacial rivers that surge across sandy wastes toward the sea; voyagers would stop at lonely farms to ask fording advice.

Even today, the Ringroad—Iceland's Highway 1, its grandest thorough-fare—regularly washes out along the south coast, as channels choked with rain or snowmelt carve new paths across the plain. Four-wheel-drive vehicles rather than horses now perform the chancy work of testing new routes, but travel off main roads remains a scary business. In July 1989, two couples with three young girls crossed a highland river in powerful jeeps. The couples were experienced backcountry drivers. Nonetheless the lead jeep, with the three girls aboard, overturned in midstream. The youngest child drowned at once, but the men rescued the other two girls and the woman from the capsized jeep. It was two days, however, before a search was launched. In the interim, the woman and children died of hypothermia.

Especially as regards overland travel, the importance of horses to the early settlers cannot be exaggerated. The first horses were brought in large numbers from western Norway and the British Isles. With their aid, men often forded bone-chilling rivers they could not have swum. After eleven centuries, the Icelandic horse has a masterly inbred technique for fording. In fast water, he will swim cocked slightly on his side, with his legs pointing downstream, allowing the rider, who floats just upstream, to hold the mane as the horse tows him across.

Although they are no longer indispensable to the economy—one of their chief uses nowadays is to give tourists trailrides—the horses of Iceland still command the countryside (there are 60,000 of them, or roughly one for every four citizens). Compared to horses elsewhere, the Icelandic breed is small, thin-legged, full-maned, graceful, and docile (they do not easily spook). They were never bred for hauling carts or carrying loads, but were, and are, a delight to ride. Driving across the country, you will see horses moving in the *tölt* or fifth gait, an odd running walk so smooth the rider's head does not bob; no other horse in the world still accomplishes this gait, which has been lost in Europe due to breeding. Further, they have an exquisite sense of direction, revealed in the numerous cases of steeds that, having been sold from one part of the country to another, run away from their new pastures and cross great distances to return to their old farms.

The Icelandic horse has an even purer pedigree than the Icelander himself. For more than eight hundred years, no horses have been imported into the country. A horse may be sold abroad, but once it has left Iceland, it can never return.

For all their dependence on the horse, the first settlers had no great sentimental reverence for the beast. To be sure, horse-stealing was a capital crime. But one of the favorite entertainments during the Saga Age was the horsefight, a vicious spectacle in which stallions regularly killed or mutilated one another and occasionally maimed their handlers. Among the most controversial reforms that Christianity brought to Iceland was a prohibition on eating horsemeat. Writes Sigurður Magnússon:

> In a sense, the fight for Christianity in the North was a fight against the horse, against its worship and the eating of horsemeat. In some parts of Iceland, the fear or abhorrence of this heathen practice has struck such deep roots that to this very day people refuse to touch horsemeat, while in other parts it is relished. The writer knows several people who have literally gone out and vomited when informed that a week earlier they had unwittingly eaten horsemeat.

One of the pithiest and most dramatic of the sagas, *Hrafnkel's Saga*, pivots upon a horse named Freyfaxi, after the god of fertility Frey, a kind of Norse Pan. Hrafnkel loves his "pale-dun stallion, with a black mane and a black stripe down his back" so dearly that he vows to kill anyone who rides Freyfaxi without his permission. With the inevitability of a Greek tragedy, Hrafnkel's shepherd rides Freyfaxi. The author knows horses, and his descriptions of their behavior add an unerring authenticity to the dark tale. After the shepherd has performed his illicit ride, "Freyfaxi was all running with sweat; and every hair on his body was dripping. He was covered in mud and panting with exhaustion. He rolled over a dozen times, and then neighed loudly and started to race down the path." Thus, Hrafnkel guesses the truth: he slays the shepherd, setting in motion the terrible conclusion of the whole saga.

To the pagan Icelander, the horse played many roles in addition to its functional life. Horses were considered descendants of the gods, and as such, they were ambivalent figures, capable of both good and evil. The kelpie, a mainstay of old Icelandic folk tales, was a malevolent horse that lived in rivers. A real, though dead, horse had a place in a Viking curse: one who wished to jinx his enemies would erect a "scorn-pole." Atop an upright shaft of wood he would plant a horse's head. *Egil's Saga* describes its hero's curse upon the king and queen of Norway: "Here I set up a pole of insult against King Eirík and Queen Gunnhild." Egil then turns the horse head toward the mainland: "And I direct this insult against the guardian spirit of this land, so that every one of them shall go astray, neither to figure nor find their dwelling places until they have driven King Eirík and Queen Gunnhild from this country." Shortly thereafter, the saga relates, the rulers are forced from the throne.

Almost as important as the horse is the sheepdog, whose role continues to be vital in a country where ninety percent of the livestock are sheep. With his thick golden fur, perky ears, and penchant for dashing wildly about, he remains a relatively pure Icelandic breed. Dogs figure often in the sagas. Along with hunting and herding sheep, they guard their masters' houses. In

OVERLEAF: ICELANDIC PUREBREDS, WITH THEIR SHAGGY MANES AND THIN LEGS, MOVE IN THE TÖLT GAIT, A SMOOTH RUNNING WALK THEY ARE THE ONLY HORSES IN THE WORLD STILL TO PERFORM.

*Njál's Saga*, Gunnar is protected by a formidable dog named Sam, who sits on the roof keeping watch. As they plan their attack, one of Gunnar's enemies tells another that it will be futile to attack Gunnar in his home: "that is quite impossible as long as the dog is alive." The necessary first step of the ambush, then, is to lure Sam from the roof and kill him. Inside the house, Gunnar wakes to hear the dog's death moan. With laconic foreboding, he says, "You have been harshly treated, Sam, my fosterling. It may well be fated that my turn is coming soon."

On the voyages of settlement, the Vikings carried horses, cattle, and sheep in their *hafskips*. For eight centuries, cattle outnumbered sheep in Iceland, until they had so overgrazed the land that their numbers began to dwindle. Today there are about 60,000 cattle in Iceland, compared to 900,000 sheep in the winter and some two million during the early summer lambing season. Remarkably, even the cattle and sheep are virtually purebred Icelandic strains, recognizably different from their European cousins. The sheep, for instance, has the short tail and pure white coat of an ancient Nordic strain.

In the twelfth century, when the Vikings arrived, "Iceland was wooded from the shoreline to the mountain slope," in the words of historian Ari the Wise. The country was systematically deforested, however, as settlers cleared land for crops and grazing animals and gathered firewood. Yet even the original birch woods were inadequate for building; the settlers charac-

LEFT: THIS GEOTHERMAL STEAM VENT ERUPTS CONTINUOUSLY. DESPITE SUCH ACTIVITY, ALLUSIONS TO VOLCANIC PHENOMENA ARE SURPRISINGLY RARE IN THE ICELANDIC SAGAS.

RIGHT: SUNSET REVEALS THE FORMS OF A GROUP OF VOLCANIC PSEUDO-CRATERS BESIDE THE SHORE OF MÝVATN.

teristically brought timber from Norway to build their houses. Driftwood—trees that had floated down Russian and Scandinavian rivers and drifted for months across the arctic waters—was one of the most precious natural resources in Iceland. (So were beached whales, the spoils of which, as the sagas relate, could cause murderous feuds among claimants. The Icelandic word for godsend, *hvalreki*, translates literally as "stranded whale.")

Aside from fish and birds, which were prodigally abundant, there was little in the way of natural game in the new land. The only indigenous land mammal was the arctic fox. Wolves and snakes appear in the sagas, but they are literary conventions imported from Scandinavia, for neither creature was found in Iceland. Once in a while a polar bear trapped on an ice floe would drift in from Greenland. (This still occurs: the most recent sighting came in 1978.) There are old legends of fights between men and bears in Iceland. It was a great deed to capture a polar bear: as early as 880 a daring Viking trapped one off the Iceland coast and presented it to King Harald Finehair in Norway, starting a fashion for collecting bears among Scandinavian monarchs.

Through the analysis of historical records and geological evidence, scientists have determined that the Icelandic climate was milder from about the year 874 through the 1170s than it was for centuries thereafter. The first hundred years of settlement, which have taken on the aura of a golden age, were, therefore, easier to live in than Iceland's Dark Ages. The medieval diet was rich and varied. Meat was most highly valued, the mark of affluence: not only

OVERLEAF: A FULMAR NESTS
BENEATH THE OVERHANG
OF THE WATERFALL AT
SELJALANDSFOSS.

49

beef and mutton, but ham and bacon—pigs were imported early, though not in great numbers—and chicken and fish. (In the *Laxdaela Saga*, the hero Kjartan Óláfsson, as token of his conversion to Christianity, becomes the first man in Iceland to "dry-fast" during Lent; i.e. to go without meat. "People thought it so remarkable," says the saga, "that Kjartan could live for so long without meat that they travelled long distances just to look at him.")

The diet included also herbs, dairy products, barley, and corn, and Icelanders made their own beer, though they imported wine from Europe. By the seventeenth century, a bad time for Iceland, the pigs, poultry, barley, and corn had died out. Natives ate much less meat and more fish than they had during the tenth century; whey and *skyr* (curdled skim milk) were staple foods; and the larder was wretchedly supplemented by gathering moss, angelica roots, and seaweed such as dulse, which were prepared by boiling in milk. Starvation was not uncommon, though it had been rare during the Saga Age. Vegetable gardens were not widely cultivated until the nineteenth century. (Icelanders today eat more sugar than the inhabitants of any other country; the standard explanation is a reaction against centuries of insipid whey and dulse and the daily dose of cod liver oil.)

The difficulty of travel in early Iceland inspired a vigorous tradition of hospitality. Writes Magnússon, "For centuries it was considered the blackest of crimes not to receive a traveller and house him free of charge." This custom persisted into the 1920s. When W. G. Collingwood stayed overnight at Hliðarendi in 1897, in the house that stood on the site of Gunnar's beloved home, the farmer cleared the guest room, sanded the floor, and made up beds; then, "to suit the English fad of fresh air, a window was taken bodily out."

In 1936 W. H. Auden reported, "Nearly every farm will put you up, and though the standard of comfort of course varies, they will all do their best to make you comfortable. Prices from 4 to 6 kronur (about a dollar) a day inclusive." By now, with the rise of organized tourism, it is no longer conventional to stop at a farmhouse and ask for lodging. Instead a string of government-authorized hotels, like the paradors of Spain, rings the country on or near Highway 1. In addition, there is Icelandic Farm Holidays, a network of about 100 farms around the country that rent out rooms and fix meals for tourists. The tradition of hospitality lingers on. If you trespass up some private driveway to ask directions in rural Iceland, you will be greeted far more warmly than you would in Texas or Montana. Indeed, writing in 1977, Magnússon (who, one must remember, is Icelandic) claims that "I have frequently experienced, when travelling in remote districts, that a farmer's wife came running with a pitcher of milk, offering the travellers refreshments and sometimes even inviting them to stay overnight."

Gradually over the centuries, the balance of Iceland's economy shifted from farming to fishing. By now, seventy percent of the country's exports are fish and fish products; no other nation in the world is so dependent on its fisheries. Cod has always been the main catch. Despite the advent of fresh-frozen processing, you still find in use all over the coastline the great wooden lattices of old fish racks, each hung with thousands of salted, gutted cod drying in the sun.

But going to sea in small boats was, and remains, a perilous business: the sagas are full of shipwrecks. In the last fifty years alone, 1,300 Icelandic

HORSES AND WATERFALLS
SEEM EMBLEMATIC OF THE
ICELANDIC COUNTRYSIDE.

fishermen have died at sea. The shores are strewn with the carcasses of ships run aground, victims of the winds and storms of the fickle North Atlantic: some of them rotting wooden hulks from the nineteenth century, others spanking steel boats that met disaster within the previous few months.

The most important fishing port in Iceland is Heimaey, the only town among the fifteen jewel-like isles that make up the Vestmannaeyjar, or Westman Islands, off the dangerous south coast. With a population of merely 5,000, Heimaey brings in twelve percent of the country's fish catch. Heimaey gained the attention of the world in January 1973, when a volcano that had lain dormant for more than 5,000 years suddenly erupted. Without a single mishap, in the middle of a midwinter night virtually the entire population of the island was evacuated to the mainland. During the days that followed, nearly a third of Heimaey was buried by lava (you can still see the vestiges of a few houses, crushed by the flows, peeking out from beneath tons of cooled magma). As the lava advanced, it threatened to close off Heimaey's superb natural harbor. Experts counseled abandoning the island altogether, but scores of volunteers from the island and mainland heroically stopped the advance by pumping cooling seawater onto the molten flow. In the end, the new tongues of land actually improved the harbor.

The Westman Islands have been inhabited as long as the mainland. Archaeological evidence from a dig just west of the town of Heimaey suggests, in fact, that there were people—presumably Norse—in residence even before 874. The islands may have gotten their name from an early slave revolt. According to the *Landnámabók*, during the first generation of settlement, Ingólf Arnarson's brother Hjörleif was murdered by his Irish thralls, who then fled with their women and goods to the islands. Ingólf pursued them and took revenge, killing some and forcing others to jump off cliffs. The dead Irish slaves, however, the "Westmen," gave their name to the islands.

Many years later the Westman Islands were victimized by one of the strangest and direst catastrophes in Iceland's history. On July 16, 1627, the peaceful fishermen of Heimaey were surprised to see unfamiliar ships sail into port. They took these aliens to be Turks, but in fact they were Algerian pirates on what may have been the most northerly raid in their history. They landed, three hundred strong, screaming wild cries, and set about massacring the inhabitants. After the initial slaughter, the pirates herded together the survivors in a large storehouse. They chose two hundred forty-two of the strongest and youngest, removed them from the storehouse, then burned it to the ground with all the others inside. The captives were taken to Algiers and sold into slavery. The only survivors on the island were a handful who hid in caves; residents today will proudly show you these hideouts of desperation. Nine years after the massacre, Danes and Icelanders raised enough money to ransom thirty-nine of the slaves in Africa, but only thirteen ever returned to Iceland.

The Westman Islands are also Iceland's richest seabird colony. Fifteen different species nest here, including guillemots, fulmars, petrels, gannets, and five kinds of auk. The most numerous of all are puffins, which are as common on Heimaey as pigeons are in New York. With their psychedelic orange-and-blue beaks, triangular eye-markings, orange feet, and plump white-breasted bodies, puffins are cherished by birdwatchers everywhere as

THE LAVA FLOW IN 1973
COVERED SOME FORTY
PERCENT OF THE TOWN OF
HEIMAEY.

cute, exotic creatures, the avian equivalent of koala bears. They nest in turf burrows on cliff tops, pose on promontories for the telephoto lens, and fly like badly designed windup toys, with frantic, choppy strokes that seem barely to get them airborne. Oddly enough, puffins have never successfully been raised in captivity.

One of the great sports in Iceland is puffin hunting. For centuries, going back to the first settlers, the puffin harvest was crucial to subsistence; now it is only a pastime, albeit a highly competitive one. On the uninhabited out-islands of the Westmans, as well as on certain parts of Heimaey, hunters go out on windy days in July and August to bag their catch. These men—among them bankers and lawyers in daily life—have built cozy huts on the out-islands where they can camp for a week or two at a time, swapping tales and passing the vodka.

To catch puffins, the expert uses a net fixed at the end of a very light fiberglass pole as long as fifteen feet. He selects a ridge on a sheer sea-cliff and crouches in the grass, making himself as unobtrusive as possible. If the wind is right, puffins will regularly sail by at great speeds, anywhere from a few to fifty feet off the ground. The hunter must see one coming, swing the net high in a sudden arc, and snag the puffin in flight. It is a dangerous sport. The best perches are right at the edges of cliffs, and it's easy to get carried away with the follow-through. Quite a few experienced hunters have fallen, some to their deaths. Once he brings the puffin to earth, the hunter seizes it by the head, twists, and breaks its neck with a quick slap of the bird across his opposite forearm. He may then prop a few dead puffins upright in the grass to serve as decoys.

LEFT: PUFFINS, MEMBERS OF THE AUK FAMILY, MAKE A LIVING DIVING FOR AND SWIMMING AFTER SMALL FISH FRY AND SAND EELS. ON THE WHOLE, THEY DO SOMEWHAT BETTER AT SEA THAN IN THE AIR BECAUSE OF THEIR SHORT WINGS.

CENTER: A PUFFIN HUNTERS' CABIN ON DALFJALL, HEIMAEY. THE SPORT TODAY HAS MORE TO DO WITH MALE CAMARADERIE THAN WITH PUTTING FOOD ON THE TABLE.

RIGHT: WITH A PRECISE SWING OF HIS LONG-HANDLED NET THE HUNTER BAGS A BIRD IN MIDFLIGHT: THE ART OF THE HUNT HAS CHANGED LITTLE OVER THE CENTURIES.

Good hunters have bagged more than a thousand birds in a single day. There are so many puffins in Iceland, however (some calculate twelve million), that their numbers continue to grow despite the best efforts of the men with nets. The hunters save some birds to eat, give others to friends, and sell the rest. In fancy restaurants in Reykjavík, roast puffin is a pièce de résistance; it is dark and rich and tastes a bit like goose. Nevertheless, many Icelanders have never eaten it.

As you move east along the coast beyond the isolated port of Vík, which lies almost at the southernmost point of the mainland, the road crosses a vivid badlands of old lava flows and glacial plains. Here was some of the most treacherous traveling of all in olden days; in fact, the last stretch of the Ringroad to be completed, in 1974, was the long bridge that spans the many channels of the Skeiðará River. This waterway was so effective a barrier that even rodents such as the field mouse, which had become ubiquitous elsewhere in Iceland, never reached the land east of the Skeiðará until the bridge was built.

Farther east along this southern coast lies Skaftafell, a famous region of alpine scenery on the edge of the gigantic glacier Vatnajökull. Named a national park in 1967, it is on the grand scale, with spiky ridges rising abruptly from the plain, chaotic glacial tongues carving broad valleys, and Iceland's highest peak, Hvannadalshnúkur, looming ice-capped in the east. Yet the hiking here, on a grassy heath full of benches and hollows, is of the most genial sort, like something out of the Swiss foothills. In summer the ground teems with saxifrage and harebell, the air with redwings, snipes, and meadow pipits. Translucent brooks idle among patches of moss so bright

OVERLEAF: HELGAFELL, THE OLD CRATER ON HEIMAEY, IS A NEAR NEIGHBOR OF THE CRATER OF ELDFELL, WHICH SUDDENLY ERUPTED IN 1973.

green they look chartreuse under the sun. The canyons hide a number of small waterfalls, including the basalt wonder of Svartifoss.

There is no more picturesque area in Iceland. Yet just as in the Middle Ages the Alps themselves were considered hideous, a place to shun, so the region around Skaftafell was regarded as a no-man's-land during the Saga Age. Svinafell, the ancient farmstead on the edge of the national park, was the place from which Flosi Thórðarsson came, the man who planned and carried out the Burning in Njál's Saga, and who later supposedly leapt the chasm at Thingvellir to escape his pursuers. In the saga, his dwellingplace seems to stand on a wild frontier, almost at the eastern limit of the known world.

The sagas in general regard the interior of Iceland with indifference at best, horror at worst. Here is wilderness in the old sense of the word—a place where men are lost, bewildered. Whenever a tale turns to a man living alone in the interior, the mood is sinister. In Njáls' Saga, Killer-Hrapp, fleeing his enemies, comes across a solitary man named Tofi who has built his house in a forest clearing. Hrapp confesses the murder he has committed, saying, "Let's not beat about the bush....I know that we are both scoundrels, because you would not be burying yourself away here unless you were on the run from somebody yourself." Tofi confesses his own crime, and the two "scoundrels" decide to live together.

In Grettir's Saga, having accepted his fate as an outlaw, Grettir meets a mysterious, half-supernatural rider named Lopt, who replies to Grettir's questions in verse riddles, indicating that he lives alone near the Langjökull glacier. Later Grettir builds himself a solitary hut on the inland moor called the Arnarvatnsheiði, a place that even today is deep wilderness. His only visitors on the moor are other outlaws, some of whom he befriends, while others he kills. Still later, Grettir moves into a cave with Lopt, who has revealed himself to be a troll.

The southeast part of Iceland goes virtually unmentioned in the sagas. With its difficult coast and the Vatnajökull pressing almost to the shore, this was an umpromising land for settlement. Yet, oddly, it was here that the Vikings found most of the papar, the Irish monks who had preceded them. According to the historian G. J. Marcus, this was "a currach coast" par excellence: irregular, deeply indented, with a heavy swell and strong tidal currents, like the west coast of Ireland where the monks had learned their sea-craft.

One of their former settlements is given away by the name Papós, clearly related to the name for the Irish hermit. A long barrier island creates a bay of calm, above which stark, talus-covered mountains hover. It seems even today as spartan a place as the most devout anchorite could wish. If you ask directions in English at the only farmhouse in the area, the shy family living there will stare back uncomprehending. (Although in Reykjavík virtually everybody speaks English, in the rural outback this is the exception rather than the rule.) They soon get the drift, however, and direct you to Papós by pointing and pantomime.

Beside the shore stand the obvious nineteenth-century ruins of a fishing station and a boarding school, with their stone walls, weathered boards, and iron spikes. Walk a hundred yards inland and you will find, almost lost in the tundra, the outlines of ancient foundations. Where the stream has undercut the grassy bank, collapsed stone walls lie bare. From such vestigial traces,

PLOVER EGGS NESTLE IN THE ALPINE TUNDRA OF SKAFTAFELL.

fantasies spring. The monks may have brought sheep and goats with them, as they did to the Faroe Islands. Did they also try to plant crops, or did they fill their starving bellies with seaweed? How did they fish? Did they venture inland, and if so, why? Deprived of most things we call human, did they sit on the shore and stare into tempests, conjuring trances in which they beheld the miraculous visions with which the *immrama*, the old accounts of the *currach* voyages, abound?

The east of Iceland is a vast and varied place, today the least-visited part of the country. A cluster of towns, including Egilsstaður and Neskaupstaður, gives it a nucleus of civilization, but much of the countryside is empty. The Eastfjords, where the coast-hugging road winds tortuously in and out of one deep inlet after another, are dominated by hulking mountains that shade reticent farmsteads. Inland the country is gentle, a tapestry of broad valleys and boggy upland moors. On the south shore of the Lögurinn, a serene lake that is fifteen miles long but little more than a mile across, lies the Hallormsstaðaskógur, the largest remaining forest in Iceland. A tangle of downy birch, rowan, and tea-leaved willow, these woods give a feeling of what, if Ari the Wise is correct, most of Iceland must have looked like in 874.

This is the country of *Hrafnkel's Saga*, the tragedy of the overproud chieftain who loved his horse Freyfaxi more than a man should. Whoever wrote the saga was acutely familiar with the local landscape, for the tale is full of geographic detail. When Hrafnkel goes to the Althing, the author tells us his exact route and that the journey took seventeen days. Of trails across the

LEFT: DESPITE THE PROXIMITY OF THE VATNAJÖKULL GLACIER, THE ALPS AROUND SKAFTAFELL ABOUND WITH BIRDS AND FLOWERING PLANTS, INCLUDING ESPECIALLY ARCTIC COTTON.

CENTER: A HIGH RIDGECREST IN SKAFTAFELL, ICELAND'S MOST POPULAR NATIONAL PARK.

RIGHT: THE SVARTIFOSS, A SMALL WATERFALL, SPILLS OVER A CLIFF OF PERFECT BASALT COLUMNS IN SKAFTAFELL.

swampy moor that lies just west of the Lögurinn, he writes:

> Fljótsdalsheiði is stony and boggy and difficult to travel over, yet Hrafnkel and his father used to visit each other frequently, for they were on very affectionate terms. Hallfreð thought the usual path across the moor was much too rough, so he looked for an alternative route south of the hills which rise on the moor, and there he found a drier but slightly longer way. This path has been called Hallfreðargata ever since, and it can only be used by those who are thoroughly familiar with the moor.

Although most of the northeast is little-visited, the region around Mývatn, Iceland's fourth-largest lake, is a favorite wildlife retreat. The lake itself is the breeding grounds for more ducks than are found anywhere else in Iceland—and also more insects, as the name ("Lake of Midges") indicates. But what chiefly attracts visitors is the prodigies of vulcanism rampant in the area. Just east of the Námafjall, a bleak plain is strewn with burping gray mudpots, shrill steam vents, and sandbanks puffing sulphurous fumes. You cannot help being reminded of Yellowstone, but here there are no rangers or guard rails—instead, a sign in five languages warns you to walk only on brown earth, not white, gray, or yellow, through which unwary hikers have been known to plunge to a scalding denouement. Just to the north is Krafla, a mountain that blew sky high in 1975 and that is expected to erupt again soon. Near Mývatn the Dimmuborgir unfolds its collection of grotesque towers, humps, and crevices in jet-black congealed lava.

OVERLEAF: A WISP OF GEOTHERMAL STEAM RISES OVER LAKE MÝVATN AT DAWN.

The sagas do not mention Mývatn. Perhaps to the early settlers, this region, like Skaftafell, was simply a wasteland, where what today seems nature's magnificence looked only freakish and rude. Indeed, as late as 1862, the English writer Sabine Baring-Gould, who loved mountain scenery, could feel only disgust among the mudpots east of Námafjall, which he memorably described:

> In some, the mud is thick as treacle, in others it is simply ink-black water. The thundering and throbbing of these boilers, the thud, thud of the hot waves chafing their barriers, the hissing and splattering of the smaller fumaroles, the plop-plop of the little mudpools, and above all, the scream of a steam-whistle at the edge of a blue slime-pond, produce an effect truly horrible.

Yet given the preponderance of volcanic phenomena in Iceland, it is puzzling that the sagas scarcely refer to such things. The island does seem to have grown more active after the Middle Ages, but even so, the pioneers must have been forcibly struck by the amount of terrain that lay covered in lava. One of the rare allusions to volcanic activity comes from an old story about the debate in the year 1000, when the Althing was deciding whether to adopt Christianity as Iceland's official religion. In the midst of the deliberations, a man came running to report that a new eruption of "earth-fire" was endangering the farmstead of one of the chieftains. The pagans began to mutter, "It is no wonder that the gods are angry at such speeches." Snorri Goði (who tends to get the last word in most of the sagas in which he appears) rejoined, "What were the gods angry at, when the lava on which we now stand was burning here?"

PRECEDING PAGES: AT 6,950 FEET, HVANNADALSHNÚKUR CROWNS ICELAND. IN ANCIENT TIMES, ONLY OUTLAWS VENTURED ONTO THE GREAT WASTELANDS OF THE ICECAPS.

If any part of Iceland is ugly, it tends to be the small towns. Since World War I, the building material of choice has been corrugated iron, which lends itself to a mundane architecture. Auden was unimpressed even by Reykjavík: "My first impression of the town was Lutheran, drab and remote." For more than a millennium before the war, the Icelandic house had been built of turf and wood. A few turf farmsteads have been preserved as museums. One of the best is at Laufás, on a meadow above the Eyjafjörður in the north.

This former parsonage, which housed from twenty to thirty people at a time, consists of a low complex of interconnected turf rooms. Each had its own function: there was a dairy, a weaving room, a *dúnhús* devoted solely to cleaning birds, and a seldom-used *brúðarhús* for dressing a bride before her wedding. The center of the house was the *baðstófa*, a combination living room and bedroom.

Laufás vividly conveys what life was like in rural Iceland before the twentieth century. On a sunny day, the small, earthen-smelling rooms seem snug, and the whole parsonage has a vernacular beauty, both inside and out, that instantly strikes the eye. Life here, however, as in every turf farm, was often miserable. If the roof were not pitched at exactly the right angle, it would crack or leak. When rain got inside, the floor turned to mud. The turf grew cobwebbed and mildewy; disease was common. Smoke from oil lamps fogged the close air. In the single *baðstófa* slept as many as twenty-five people, two to a bed. Old hay or seaweed served for the mattress. Even in winter, body heat was the only source of warmth. Baring-Gould, who stayed in many turf farms in 1862, complained about the lice that "teem in the unwholesome recesses of the *bathstófa*."

II-35

LEFT: MOST TURF FARMS HAD A DÚNHÚS—A ROOM DEVOTED SOLELY TO THE PLUCKING AND CLEANING OF BIRDS—LIKE THIS ONE AT LAUFÁS.

CENTER: UNTIL THE TWENTIETH CENTURY, VIRTUALLY ALL HOUSES IN ICELAND LOOKED LIKE THIS ABANDONED TURF HOMESTEAD AT HVALNES, ON THE SOUTHEAST COAST.

RIGHT: A CHARACTERISTIC ROOF-PEAK TOPS THE TURF FARM OF LAUFÁS IN THE NORTH, BUILT BETWEEN 1853 AND 1882 AND PRESERVED AS A MUSEUM TODAY.

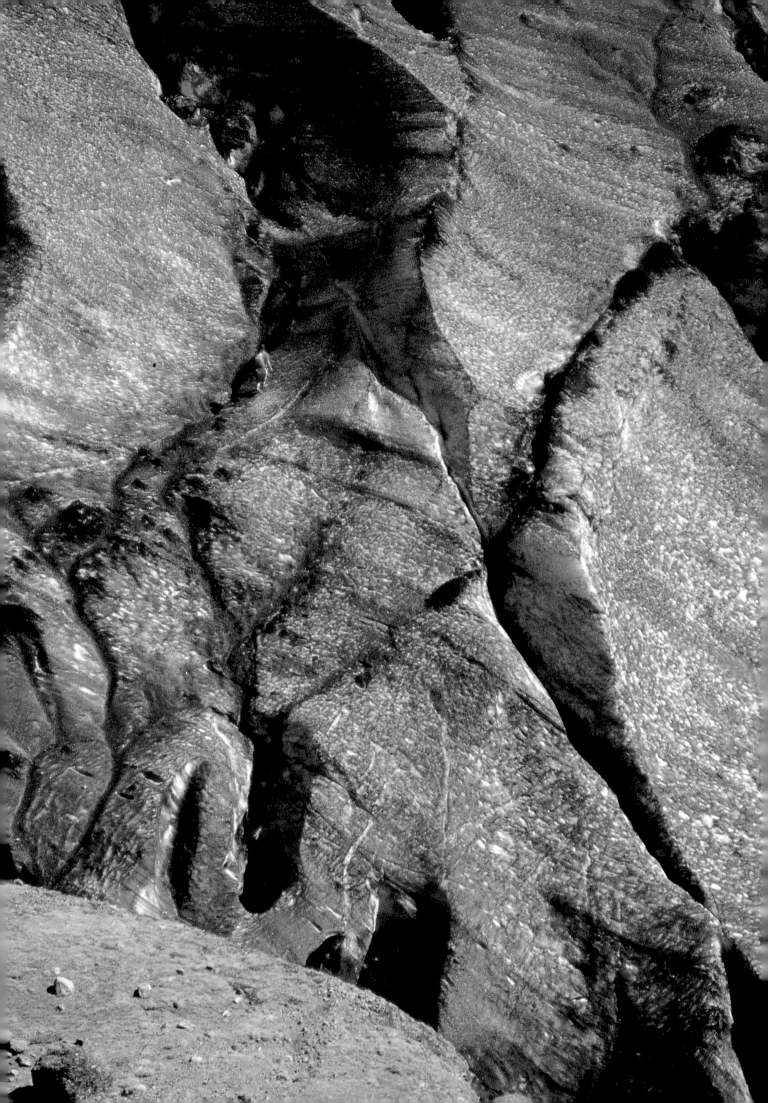

Unlike the Icelanders of the genus *homo*, these horrible parasites are endowed with a predilection for novelty, and in a moment scent out the blood of an Englishman, and come in eager hordes, from which he finds no escape till he reaches a boiling spring in which he can plunge his clothes and annihilate his tormentors wholesale. Curiously enough, the natives have a superstitious dread of killing one of these constant companions, and they will remove one which is particularly obnoxious, and lay it gently on the table, without for a moment thinking of depriving it of life.

The design of such turf farms as Laufás goes far back in history. We know little about houses in the Saga Age, but we do know that they were different in crucial respects, and they may well have been superior to what came later. The medieval *skáli*, or longhouse, was not a prairie-dog burrow of connecting rooms, but a single structure of quite lofty dimensions—as large as one hundred feet by twenty feet. The *baðstófa* evolved out of a kind of sauna—a luxury that a country still rich in firewood could afford.

To imagine daily life in Iceland during its Dark Ages, you need only sit for a while in the baðstófa at Laufás, as the dim light of midday filters through the tiny windows high in the wall. Replace that light with the flickering glow of an oil lamp, and listen to the January wind shrieking around a corner in the darkness outside. About you are ranged the taciturn men of the household, smoking their pipes, combing wool, making horsehair ropes. The women sit spinning and sewing.

Yet tonight, piercing the seamless boredom of the Icelandic winter, an air of expectation holds the family in its sway. The stranger there, brushing the snow from his boots, is that most marginal of vagabonds, the itinerant reciter. Tonight, in exchange for a bed and a meal, he will fill the evening hours by repeating the sagas from memory. Even the children are alert with anticipation, for there is no more cherished occasion.

In such a fashion over the centuries, the tales of the Saga Age became the heritage of a nation.

A SUMMER CLIMBER MAKES HIS WAY PAST THE SERACS AND CREVASSES OF THE VATNAJÖKULL. THE DARK COLOR COMES FROM ROCK DEBRIS CARRIED ATOP THE MOVING ICE.

LAVA BADLANDS SURROUND
AN OASIS OF SETTLEMENT
IN THE NORTHEAST AT
MÖÐRUDALUR—THE HIGHEST
FARM IN ICELAND, ON A
FRIGID PLATEAU AT 1,540 FEET.

# LEAVES OF VELLUM AND THE CLIFFS OF DRANGEY

W

HEN THEY FIRST CAME TO ICELAND AT THE END OF THE
ninth century, the Norwegians, in common with their Scandinavian neighbors, lacked a true written language. They did
inscribe runes in stone, wood, and metal. These mysterious,
quasi-alphabetic mottos have never been completely deciphered. This is
not to say that the Norse were an unliterary people. Some of the trenchant
poems that were later written down by Icelandic scribes may have been
composed as early as the ninth century and preserved by oral tradition. The
poet, or scald, as he was called, was an honored figure in Viking society.
Many of the sagas incorporate, in the mouths of heroes and warriors, highly
formal verses that we have good reason to believe were composed during
the Saga Age. The model is Egil Skallagrímsson, whose "Lament for My
Sons" is one of the most moving poems in Icelandic.

Runes were usually carved either to commemorate a person or event or to
invest an object such as a sword or a necklace with special power. Their
magical charm is underscored by the Norse myth of their origin: Óðin, the
High One among the gods, mastered the meaning of runes only by hanging
for nine nights from a windy tree—this, after he had been wounded by a
spear. In the town of Borgarnes, atop the mound that marks the grave of
Skallagrím Kveldúlfsson (Egil's father), there is a slab of granite carved with
runes. Near this place in 1897 Collingwood sketched what he was told was
the only surviving runestone in Iceland. He thought he could read its
inscription as "Here sleeps the hero, Kjartan, son of Óláf," but scholars

73

doubt that the great warrior and lover of the *Laxdaela Saga*, "the handsomest of all men ever born in Iceland," lies buried here—if indeed he ever existed. (What is more, the stone that Collingwood sketched is not the same as the fragment that rests in Borgarnes today.)

The magical power of runes plays an important role in the sagas. Having erected his scorn-pole against the rulers of Norway, Egil inscribes his formulaic curse in runes on the wooden post. Similarly, runes carved by a witch on a piece of driftwood seal the doom of Grettir the Strong.

It was only around 1100, a century after the formal adoption of Christianity, that Icelanders began to write their own language. One of the first books was a short history of the country, called *Íslendingabók*, written by Ari the Wise before 1130. The fact that in this seminal work Ari, who had been educated in the church, chose to write in Icelandic and not Latin is highly surprising—and as crucial to the course of Icelandic literature as Dante's choosing Italian for the *Divine Comedy* was to the Renaissance.

During the next two centuries, Icelandic literature grew and flourished. That a new country of only some 70,000 inhabitants should yield a galaxy of brilliant works, while such older, wealthier, and more populous neighbors as Norway and Sweden produced nothing that remotely compares, remains an inexplicable mystery. The English critic W. P. Ker, praising the sagas, touches on this paradox:

> The material life of Iceland in the Middle Ages was barbarous when compared to the life of London or Paris, not to speak of Provence or Italy, in the same centuries ....[Yet] the record of that life is by a still greater interval in advance of all the common modes of narrative then known to the more fortunate or more luxurious parts of Europe.

Second only to the sagas as a body of great writing was the Icelandic poetry of the age. Many of the finest heroic and narrative poems were collected in a book called the *Elder Edda* (the origin of the name *edda* is itself uncertain). These include the famous *Völuspa*, a cosmogony of the Norse gods, and the pithy *Hávamál*, or "The Words of the High One" (Óðin). The dry aphorisms and aperçus of the latter can often stand alone:

Who travels widely needs his wits about him,
   The stupid should stay at home.

To a false friend the footpath winds
   Though his house be on the highway;
To a sure friend there is a short cut,
   Though he live a long way off.

For these things give thanks at nightfall:
The day gone, a guttered torch,
A sword tested, the troth of a maid,
Ice crossed, ale drunk.

Old Icelandic poetry does not rhyme, nor does it usually fall into syllable-counting meters such as iambic pentameter. It depends rather on a fixed number of heavy accents in each line, and on alliteration among these accented syllables. Anyone who has studied Anglo-Saxon poetry will be familiar with the principle. (The above translations, by W. H. Auden, imitate the effect in English: e.g., "For *thése things* give *thánks* at *níghtfall*."/)

A separate poetic tradition, of which many examples have come down to us, is scaldic verse. These short, highly contorted stanzas put a premium on cleverness, indirect allusion, and formal pyrotechnics; they seem as much riddles as poems. Their stock in trade is the kenning, a rhetorical device that goes back beyond Homer. To call a camel a "ship of the desert" is to use a kenning; Norse poets conventionally called a ship a "horse of the sea." Scaldic verse is difficult to read, even for intellectual Icelanders; it is impossible to translate. By way of illustration, the leading scholar of medieval Icelandic literature, Jónas Kristjánsson, offers an extremely literal rendering of a classic scaldic verse:

> The god of the mail-shirt
> suspends the ringing noose of the fist-tongs
> on the hawk-trodden
> gallows of the falcon.
> I raise the cord of the gallows-beam of the shield-wearier
> on the gibbet-bar of spear-storm.
> The feeder of battle-hawks
> commands all the more praise.

With its obscure kennings, the poem is incomprehensible, unless one knows that "god of the mail-shirt" and "feeder of battle-hawks" mean warrior, "ringing noose of the fist-tongs" and "cord of the gallows-beam of the shield-wearier" mean bracelet, and so on. The verse, by Egil Skallagrímsson himself (generally conceded to be the greatest of the scaldic poets), describes the king of England's passing a treasured bracelet on the tip of his sword to Egil, who accepts it.

It is hard for today's reader to find pleasure in such arcane wordplay, but in the Middle Ages a scald could hold a royal court spellbound with his verses. Much of the skill lay in fitting a thought into a tight and arbitrary formal pattern. (A good analogue is the limerick, as tight a verse form as English allows, the wit of which depends on the poet's following a prescribed meter and rhyme scheme.) A scald was also supposed to be good at improvisation. In a famous scene in Egil's Saga, the hero, sentenced to die in the morning by Eirík of Norway, saves his life by amusing the king with the long scaldic poem he has stayed up all night composing. In Kristjánsson's wry appraisal, "It's a rather simple poem, which is understandable, as he had not so much time to write it."

In his late sixties, Kristjánsson is director of the Árni Magnússon Institute in Reykjavík, where most of the priceless manuscripts containing Iceland's medieval literature are housed. Virtually none of these manuscripts dates from before the fourteenth century: the sagas, Edda, chronicles, and codices of law have come down to us mainly in copies, or even copies of copies, making the textual history of the Icelandic classics a matter so snarled that scholars will never untangle its knots. Still, to watch Kristjánsson lovingly turn over in his hands a battered relic such as the Grayskin manuscript of Njál's Saga—its leaves made of vellum, its cover of sealskin, and dating from 1300, only some twenty years after the saga was composed—is to feel the numinous authority these beautiful handmade, illuminated books possess.

A great deal of Iceland's medieval literature came close to vanishing for good. Once books printed on paper became widely available, the old vellum manuscripts were held in such low esteem that they were sometimes cut up

OVERLEAF: GRETTIR'S LIFT: ACCORDING TO THE SAGA, THE GREAT OUTLAW HOISTED THIS BOULDER ONE DAY TO DEMONSTRATE HIS STRENGTH TO HIS FRIENDS. A VICTORIAN TRAVELER ESTIMATED THAT IT WEIGHED TWENTY TONS.

to make patterns for clothes, or even, in times of poverty, used to make clothing and shoes themselves. Shortly after the turn of the eighteenth century, a scholar named Árni Magnússon made it his personal crusade to save the old books. For ten years he traveled through rural Iceland, buying whatever manuscripts he could lay his hands on, at whatever cost. In 1720 he sent fifty-five crates of books to the University of Copenhagen, where he set up an archive devoted to the study of medieval Icelandic literature.

More than two centuries later, when Denmark granted Iceland full independence, the most bitter and protracted sticking-point in the negotiations had to do with the dispensation of these manuscripts. Danish authorities dragged their feet for another twenty-seven years, and it was not until 1971 that a final transfer of the documents was made. Reykjavík residents now in their twenties vividly recall being taken to the harbor by their parents to see the ship arrive from Copenhagen. The children waved Icelandic flags and wore buttons that read, "Handritin heim"—"the manuscripts are home."

Although we have texts of about forty of the Sagas of Icelanders, others are lost; we know of their existence from tantalizing allusions to them in surviving works. The works of poetry and history from medieval Iceland are by now perused mainly by serious students. The sagas, however, remain instantly accessible works, read by the masses even outside Iceland. The Penguin edition of Njál's Saga in English, for instance, has sold well more than 100,000 copies since it appeared in 1960.

Growing up on a farm in the northeast, Kristjánsson first read the sagas at age seven, after his grandfather gave him a handsome collection of them and taught him to read the old orthography. (Such an initiation to the sagas was fairly normal for a young Icelander, not precocious.) "I read them all that year and the next year," says the scholar today, smiling. "I knew them better then than I do now!"

If the language in the scaldic verses reaches heights of contortion, the style of the sagas is admirably plain and straightforward. For the Icelandic reader, there is a certain archaic flavor in the phrasing, which only adds piquancy. William Morris, the great Victorian fantasist and traveler, fell in love with all things Icelandic, and set out, in collaboration with an eminent native scholar, to translate many of the sagas into English. Morris overestimated the quaintness of the language and rendered the prose in an anachronistic English hodgepodge that, while all but unreadable, still has a certain pre-Raphaelite verve of its own. Here is a specimen passage, about a ghost-haunting, from the Eyrbyggja Saga, as Englished by Morris in 1892:

> But so great trouble befell from this that no man durst feed his flocks up in the dale. Oft too was heard huge din abroad at Hvamm, and they were ware withal that the hall was ofttimes ridden. And when the winter came on Thórólf was seen home at the house many a time, and troubled the good wife the most. And great hurt gat many from this, but she herself was well-nigh witless thereat; and such was the end of it all, that the good wife died from these troublings....

Here is the same passage, translated more conventionally by Paul Schach in 1959:

> Matters became so bad that no man dared graze his livestock up in the valley. Often during the night people at Hvamm heard loud noises outside. They also often heard how the house was being ridden. And when winter came, Thórólf often appeared inside the house at the farm; and he molested the mistress of the

house most of all. Many a person took harm from this, and she herself almost went mad; and it ended with the mistress of the house dying from these apparitions.

What kind of works, in fact, are the sagas? They represent, claims the American scholar Jesse Byock, an "anomalous" literature: "They are not folktales, epics, romances, or chronicles, but mostly realistic stories about everyday issues confronting Icelandic farmers and their chieftains." What animates every saga, the motivating thread that runs through it from start to finish, is feud. "The tempers of the men," writes W. P. Ker, "are easily stirred.... The trial of a man's patience...may come from anything—horses, sheep, hay, women, merchandise. From these follow any number of secondary or retaliatory insults, trespasses, and manslaughters. Anything almost is enough to set the play going. What the matter in dispute may be, is almost indifferent to the author of the story. Its value depends on the persons; it is what they choose to make it."

Readers hoping to revel in the enchantments of Arthurian romance will be disappointed. There are no scarlet ensigns or gowns of gold lace in the Icelandic sagas, and love is treated with the same matter-of-factness as eating or drinking. At the same time, the apparent brutality of this northern world—the willingness of men to kill one another on the most trifling of pretexts—repels and even horrifies some readers. The analogy is often made, not inaptly, between the sagas and American westerns.

There are many vivid characters and events in the sagas, but readers whose expectations are based on the modern novel will likewise be disappointed. The plots are ungainly, rambling, often disunified, with casts of players so large that recent editions usually add glossaries listing the actors and family trees to keep the kinships straight. Few characters develop or change during the story. Although the author pretends a kind of omniscience, moving at will from one scene to another, he does not usually tell us what his characters are thinking; instead he uses dialogue to reveal inner thoughts. Many of these traits, of course, which may be felt as limitations by the modern reader, are the common property of most Western literature from before the eighteenth century.

Wherein lies the lasting and universal appeal, then, of the sagas? In their very plainness, their attention to detail, these narratives carry a plausibility that the best novels are at pains to duplicate. Despite their refusal to probe internally, the best saga authors have a grasp of character and motivation that is deeply wise. One of the marvels of the sagas is that, even though they were written during Iceland's third Christian century, they remain thoroughly pagan in outlook and spirit. Surfeited with the stylized artificiality of Christian romance, the student of medieval literature turns to the heathen bluntness of the sagas with a sigh of relief. In every saga, hovering above the human world, controlling even the supernatural, is the Norse idea of Fate. This frequently gives the action the stern inevitability of Greek tragedy. Just as, knowing full well the outcome, we watch fascinated as Oedipus hunts his own doom, so are we riveted by the tiny increments of plot that lead Njál to his Burning, Grettir to his ambush.

"It is no small part of the force of the Sagas," writes W. P. Ker, "and at the same time a difficulty and an embarrassment, that they have so much of reality behind them." The embarrassment comes from conventions such as the genealogies even the most minor characters are tagged with. Thórhall Grímsson occupies only a few pages of *Grettir's Saga*. Nonetheless, as he is introduced, we are patiently told, "Thórhall was the son of Grím, who was the son of Thórhall, the son of Friðmund, who was the original settler of Forsaeludale. Thórhall Grímsson had a wife called Guðrun; their son Grím and daughter Thurid were growing up at this time." No modern reader can care much about such information; yet it is this very sort of thing that gives the sagas their air of authenticity, that led centuries of readers to assume they recorded historical fact. The reason for such tedious recitations is clear. As Ker puts it, "It could not be otherwise in a country like Iceland; a community of neighbors (in spite of distances and difficulties of travelling) where there was nothing much to think about or to know except other people's affairs."

Thus we must put up with each character's genealogy, with the most finicky geographical detail, but by the same token we get an unprecedented richness of glorious fact: how hay was made in the tenth century, what it was like to ride horseback through belly-deep snowdrifts, what men ate during famines, how beggar women served as messengers and spies, what caused ships to get lost at sea. Among the sagas' other achievements, they provide, in Jesse Byock's words, "the most comprehensive extant portrayal of a Western medieval society."

The knottiest question about the sagas is how reliable they are as history. They have always been so read by Icelanders, and are today. In the town of Sauðárkrókur today, even the teenagers who listen to Michael Jackson on their Walkmans have no doubt that Grettir the Strong was a real person who met his death on that island out in the bay. Through most of the nineteenth

LEFT: THE JÓNSBÓK, A CODEX OF LAWS INSCRIBED ON ILLUMINATED PAGES, WAS THE MOST WIDELY READ ICELANDIC BOOK IN THE THIRTEENTH AND FOURTEENTH CENTURIES.

CENTER: THE SUMMIT MEADOW OF DRANGEY SEEMS AS GENTLE AS ITS PRECIPICES ARE STERN. AT THIS SOUTHWESTERN CORNER OF THE ISLAND IS HAERING'S LEAP, WHERE GRETTIR'S BROTHER ILLUGI CHASED A NORWEGIAN ATTACKER AND FORCED HIM TO JUMP TO HIS DEATH.

RIGHT: JÓNAS KRISTJÁNSSON, DIRECTOR OF THE ÁRNI MAGNÚSSON INSTITUTE AND ICELAND'S LEADING SCHOLAR OF MEDIEVAL LITERATURE, SHARES HIS KNOWLEDGE OF THE FAMOUS GRAYSKIN MANUSCRIPT OF NJÁL'S SAGA.

century, the scholarly view was that the sagas, though much embroidered by spurious episodes and literary touches, represented the work of scribes who, at the end of a long oral tradition, were writing down tales essentially grounded in history.

It may seem odd, given the great pride Icelanders feel about the sagas, that the twentieth-century reaction against that view was led by a group of native scholars called the Icelandic school. But the very idea that these old tales might be based on fact had become linked with the notion that they represented a "primitive" oral culture's naive attempt at history. Did the sagas deal with nothing grander than, in one scholar's famous sneer, "farmers at fisticuffs?" The revisionism of the Icelandic school, then, aimed to dignify the sagas as consciously crafted works of fiction, worthy of comparison with the medieval classics of Italy, France, and England.

The whole matter remains completely up in the air. It counts for little nowadays to point out, for instance, that Njál and Gunnar are mentioned in the *Landnámabók*: scholars will argue that that apparently sober compendium of data about 430 early settlers is itself a deliberate fiction.

After two centuries of intense scholarship, the most basic questions are unanswered. Kristjánsson sums up the state of our ignorance:

> We cannot identify the author of a single saga, despite more-or-less plausible attributions to named men proposed by scholars in modern times. Neither do we know for sure when and where sagas were written, although again various conjectures have been offered….We do not know what matter in them comes from oral tradition and what from the imagination of the authors. And although we assume the existence of oral traditions, we do not know what they were like.

Several of the sagas are set in the north of Iceland. The Eyjafjörður, a perfect bay in the middle of the north coast, was first settled by Helgi the Lean, who figures in a number of tales. Choosing a hot spring for his dwelling-place, Helgi named it Kristnes, for he was that rarity, a Christian among the first generation of settlers. However, says the *Landnámabók*, "He believed in Christ, but prayed to Thór when he was at sea or in difficulties."

In a splendid setting on the west shore of the Eyjafjörður lies the town of Akureyri, with a population of 14,000. For more than a century Akureyri has been the second-largest town in Iceland; it is today the only place besides Reykjavík with cosmopolitan ambitions. Its natives brag about its weather, which is warmer and drier in summer than that of the drizzly southwest. Auden in 1936 thought it "a much nicer town than Reykjavík." In 1862, Baring-Gould was amused to report:

> Akureyri is famous for possessing the largest tree in Iceland; this is a mountain ash, outside Mr. Havsteen's [a Danish merchant's] drawing-room window. It is twenty-six feet high, a straggling fellow without much foliage, overtopping the roof to which, during the winter, its branches are secured by ropes. Garden seats are placed at its roots, and, on a warm summer day, the Havsteens take supper around it, and imagine themselves in the gardens of old Denmark.

The finest saga of the north, with perhaps the most dramatic narrative of all, is *Grettir's Saga*. Scholars suspect that it may also have been the last of the sagas to be composed, sometime around 1325. The germ of the story was well-known: as both a murderer and a poet, Grettir is mentioned in the *Landnámabók*.

The great strongman grew up on the homestead at Bjarg, as desolate a place today as it must have been in the ninth century. The rather skeptical couple that farms there today will show you the stone imbedded in the front field under which, according to hoary legend, Grettir's head lies buried. They will also point out Grettir's Lift, the huge boulder resting on a tableland behind the farm, which the saga tells us Grettir hoisted one day just to show off for his friends.

William Morris visited the site in 1871. With his traveling companion, Charles Faulkner, he took a respectful breather on the grass beside the great stone, which Faulkner estimated must weigh twenty tons. Nine years earlier, Baring-Gould had stopped to ask about Grettir's head, and had been showed a green mound in the yard. He paid the owner a small sum for permission to dig. A little way down he hit an unmoveable stone—no doubt the same one that lies bare today—which put a sudden halt to his archaeology.

The sagas postulate that character is fixed at a young age. Like that other wayward hero, Egil Skallagrímsson, who kills a playmate over a ball game at age six, Grettir reveals his violent streak early. "As a child," says the saga, introducing Grettir, "he was self-willed, taciturn and harsh, sardonic and mischievous." Despite his strength and athletic skill, he shirks household tasks. When his father forces him to tend the geese, the goslings are found dead; asked to rub his father's back before the fire, Grettir picks up a metal-toothed wool comb and draws blood. More ghoulishly, he flays his father's favorite horse alive, a deed the man discovers only when he strokes the horse and finds that its hide comes loose in his hand.

Yet Grettir grows up to become not simply a bully or villain. In a series of charged episodes, he battles face-to-face with a mound-dwelling ghost, a

SUN AND STORM FILL THE SKY OVER EYJAFJÖRÐUR, THE SUPERB BAY IN THE NORTH FIRST SETTLED BY HELGI THE LEAN.

bear, a she-troll, and a giant. These antagonists are more than mere sport for Grettir: each has in some way laid a spell upon the countryside, and Grettir is the only human who dares come to grips with such monsters. Thus Grettir has affinities with St. George slaying the dragon, and with Prometheus stealing fire from the gods (indeed, he steals the mound-ghost's treasure, from which a mysterious flame has been seen to rise).

As well as being a prodigious wrestler, Grettir demonstrates, as he performs these feats, a mastery of vertical terrain. He uses ropes both to descend into the mound and to plumb the bottom of a waterfall where the giant lives; in both cases, the man assigned to guard his rope becomes terrified and flees.

In Grettir's finest hour, he vows to rid a farm of the ghost of a dead shepherd, named Glám, that is haunting it.

> Terrible things happened; many men fell unconscious at the sight of him, and others lost their sanity. Soon after Christmas, people began to see him walking about the farmhouse and were terrified by him; many of them fled away. Then Glám began to sit astride the roof at night and beat it so furiously with his heels that the house came near to breaking. Soon he was walking about day and night, and men hardly found the courage to go up the valley, even on urgent business. All this was a great calamity for the people in the district.

Grettir lays a trap with himself as bait, getting into the farmer's bed and pretending to sleep. Glám comes in the middle of the night, rides the roof raucously, then enters, where Grettir seizes him. A violent struggle ensues, with Glám trying to pull Grettir out of the house. They crash through the doorway and fall to the earth, with Grettir on top.

> Outside the moonlight was bright but intermittent, for there were dark clouds which passed before the moon and then went away. At the very moment when Glám fell, the clouds cleared away, and Glám glared up at the moon. Grettir himself once said that that was the only sight he ever saw which frightened him. Then, because of exhaustion and the sight of Glám rolling his eyes so fiercely, Grettir was overcome by such a faintness that he could not draw his short sword, and so he remained there lying closer to death than to life.

Rousing himself for a last effort, Grettir cuts off Glám's head, but not before the ghost has announced his curse:

> Up until now your deeds have brought you fame, but from now on outlawry and slaughter will come your way, and most of your acts will bring you ill luck and misfortune. You will be made an outlaw and forced to live by yourself. I also lay this curse on you: you will always see before you these eyes of mine, and they will make your solitude unbearable, and this shall drag you to your death.

In Iceland, there were two kinds of legal outlawry, lesser and fuller, as voted at the Althing. Grettir had already been made a lesser outlaw, after he had killed a man who fought with him over a lost food bag. The penalty was exile from Iceland for three years. (Grettir spends his sentence in Norway.)

Now, as it must in an Icelandic saga, Glám's curse takes effect. An altruistic act of Grettir's backfires, and at the Althing, he is entangled in legal technicalities by envious chieftains, who win a verdict of full outlawry. This means that all Grettir's property is confiscated and that no one can help him leave the country or sequester him; it amounts to a death sentence, for anyone may now kill Grettir and suffer no legal consequences.

IN THE NORTHEAST, SHEEP GRAZE ATOP TURF ISLANDS THAT HAVE BEEN CREATED BY SOIL EROSION DUE, IN TURN, TO OVERGRAZING.

85

So Grettir becomes an outlaw, living by himself in the wilderness, his only companions other loners such as Lopt, the troll. Since he has no other means of survival, Grettir begins to help himself to farmers' livestock and belongings. A reward is put on his head, and more than once he thwarts ambushes; in a single fight he kills fifteen of his pursuers. But whenever Grettir tries to sleep, he sees Glám's eyes before him, and "he had become so frightened of the dark that he did not dare go anywhere alone after nightfall, because all kinds of phantoms appeared to him then." (According to Sigurður Magnússon, fear of darkness is "a common Icelandic malady.")

Icelanders have always taken *Grettir's Saga* to heart. The great outlaw, says Magnússon, "became the symbol for many centuries of his frustrated nation, whose bad luck was out of proportion with her good endowments." For more analytical readers, however, the thorough intermixing of the realistic with the supernatural in the saga has sometimes seemed a defect. Readers of this stripe prefer such sagas as *Njál's* and *Laxdaela*, in which the plot remains predominantly realistic. Among Icelandic scholars, there is even a kind of tacit embarrassment about the more overtly supernatural sagas, as if this element threatened to reduce them to the crude folktales of a superstitious people.

Yet nothing could be more Icelandic than this easy mixing of the magical with the commonplace, especially in the laconic tone (as in the passages quoted above) that treats the supernatural with the same dry realism as the mundane. A survey conducted by the psychology department of the Univer-

LEFT: SALT COD HANG DRYING IN THE SUN FROM A FISHRACK ABOVE THE EYJAFJÖRÐUR. DESPITE MODERN FISH-PROCESSING PLANTS, THESE WOODEN RACKS ARE STILL IN USE ALL OVER THE COUNTRY.

RIGHT: EASILY MASTERING THE CURRENT IN AN ICY RIVER, AN ICELANDIC HORSE CARRIES ITS CHARGE SAFELY ACROSS.

OVERLEAF: GOÐAFOSS, A
FAMOUS WATERFALL IN THE
NORTHEAST, DERIVES ITS
NAME ("GOD'S WATERFALL")
FROM AN EARLY SETTLER'S
HAVING THROWN HIS
HEATHEN IDOLS INTO
THE CURRENT TO PLEDGE
HIS CONVERSION TO
CHRISTIANITY.

sity of Iceland in 1975 found that sixty-four percent of all Icelanders had had some experience of the supernatural. Fifty-five percent found at least plausible the existence of elves and *huldufólk*, or the "hidden people" of native lore. Fifty-six percent claimed to have communicated with the dead.

As you drive around the country today, even the *Iceland Road Guide*, whose entries can be numbingly prosaic, delves occasionally into the supernatural. "On the other side of the river," it reads on one page, "there is a rock-hill called Maelishóll, which is said to be the home of fairies and more impressive than such fairy-homes usually are." "Up from the farm," indicates the guide elsewhere, "is an impressive rocky canyon, Bólugil, with many nice falls, formerly the home of trolls."

For our own culture, Walt Disney has managed to emasculate the dark powers of the Norse and Germanic netherworld, by turning trolls, elves, dwarfs, and fairies into the harmless cousins of Mickey Mouse. To the Icelander, however, there is nothing cute about a troll. Grettir's death-struggle with the she-troll is told in a nightmarish passage; the "ogress" carries "a trough in one hand and a big cleaver in the other." Grettir is forced to grapple with her in a grotesque parody of sexual embrace: "She held him so tightly to herself that he could not use either of his hands, and was forced to clasp his arms around the woman's waist." At last he gets a hand loose, cuts off the troll's arm with his short sword, and frees himself.

Hauntings were a matter of frequent concern in medieval Iceland. The modern skeptic might analyze the many tales of whole herds of livestock

suddenly dying out as mirroring epidemics whose causes men in the Middle Ages had no way of divining. If the sagas speak for reality, Iceland no less than Puritan America or Calvinist Europe sought its own solutions. In the *Eyrbyggja Saga*, after a woman named Katla has been caught working witchcraft, she is publicly stoned to death. Ghosts could appear in many forms, even as animals. People greatly feared "shapechangers," humans with the ability to assume animal forms, as werewolves do. Farmers killed by hauntings were found sprawled in fields, covered with bruises, their limbs sometimes torn from their bodies. The only way to lay a ghost for good was to cut off its head, as Grettir does to Glám.

Dreams were prophetic, and had to be interpreted. Every person also had a *fylgja*, or "fetch," a personal guardian spirit that could be seen by others only if they had second sight; the *fylgja* often appeared during crises. In the otherwise realistic *Laxdaela Saga*, a man named Thorgils is about to die. Crossing a lava field, he sees a woman walking toward him. Instead of greeting him, she turns away, uttering a verse of warning. Shortly thereafter, when he hangs his cloak on a peg to dry, the cloak speaks to him, offering another prophetic verse. The woman, and perhaps the cloak, are manifestations of Thorgils's *fylgja*, but both speak in vain: Thorgils is beheaded by an agent of his enemy as he sits counting his money.

In such a world, it is no wonder that runes and spells had magical power. When pronouncing an oath, it was vital to get the language just right. In *Grettir's Saga*, there is a magnificent passage in which a man named Hafr, who has proclaimed a truce at a local assembly, defines the penalty that shall befall the truce-breaker (the alliterative, rhythmic prose of the formula in Icelandic is deliberately archaic):

> He shall be deemed unfit to live among men, and, like a wolf, shall be an outlaw everywhere—wherever Christians go to church or heathens hold sacrifices, wherever fire burns, the earth grows, a speaking child calls his mother and a mother bears a son, wherever people kindle fires, where a ship sails, shields glitter, the sun shines, snow drifts, a Lapp goes on skis, a fir tree grows, where a falcon flies on a long summer's day with a fair breeze blowing under both wings, where the heavens turn, where lands are lived in, where the wind washes water down to the sea, where men sow seed—in all those places the trucebreaker shall be barred from churches and Christians, from heathens, from houses and holes, from every place except Hell alone.

The incantation may refer to Christians and Hell, but it is essentially pagan in spirit—and as such, just the sort of nonsense Christianity sought to overthrow. From the first years of settlement on, chieftains erected altars to their gods—in Iceland, most often Thór or Frey. We know very little about what these shrines looked like, some of which, judging from comments in the sagas, must have been substantial.

In a very few places scattered about the countryside, the barest remains of pagan altars can still be seen. They tend to be large single stones standing alone on empty moors or on tongues of land above the sea, sometimes associated with faint stone rings embedded in the soil. These boulders, still called *blótsteinnar* ("bloodstones") by the natives, characteristically have a high content of iron oxide, which gleams a dull red. The traditional belief is that they were altars for human sacrifice, though scholars doubt it. In 1872, the great traveler and writer Richard F. Burton was guided by a shepherd boy to a *blótsteinn* and a "doom-ring" on the Snaefellsnes peninsula. "Between the two," he reported uncritically, "were buried the criminals whose backs had been broken upon the stone."

These ruined altars, with, as usual, no signs recommending them to visitors as anything out of the ordinary, are easy to overlook today. Still, like the stone foundations left by the Irish *papar*, however humble or ambiguous, they speak with mute eloquence of the power of an ancient faith in a land beset with unknown perils.

No place in Iceland reflects the geographical specificity of the sagas more hauntingly than Drangey, an island in the Skagafjörður off the north coast. Here, after years of roaming the interior as an outlaw, Grettir made his last stand. No one lives on Drangey now, and no boats make scheduled stops. The best way to get there is to hire a skipper named Jón Eiríksson, who lives on a farm called Fagranes, north of Sauðárkrókur, to take you out in his fishing boat, which is named (in Icelandic) *The New Viking*. In his early sixties, Eiríksson is probably the most knowledgeable man alive about Drangey. He will show you, in fact, the depression in the meadow at Fagranes where he says Grettir's body, minus the head, lies buried. The saga does not contradict this claim.

Drangey is a small island made of dark, crumbling rock, girded on all sides by dead-vertical cliffs up to 570 feet high. Seen from the mainland at midnight, with the midsummer sun just below the horizon behind it, the sky ghostly with rose and gray cirrus, Drangey rears sharp out of the sea, a black plug of wildness in the middle distance. Grettir chose it for his refuge because it was a site with perfect natural defenses. The island belonged to twenty farmers in the Skagafjörður, who grazed some eighty sheep on its summit. Nevertheless, Drangey was so precipitous it could be climbed only with ladders. The farmers had hoisted the sheep up with ropes.

After fifteen or sixteen years of outlawry, Grettir hires a nervous local farmer to row him out to Drangey. With him go his fifteen-year-old brother Illugi, who sees the whole thing as a great adventure, and a hypochondriac slave named Glaum, who does not. Grettir plans never to leave the island, intending to live off the sheep and the abundant seabirds that nest on the cliffs. By hauling up the top ladder, he can prevent anyone sneaking up to the summit.

Drangey must be one of the eeriest places in the world. It is guarded on the south by the Kerling ("Crone"), a twisted black pinnacle one hundred fifty feet high that springs abruptly from the sea, covered with birds and splashed white with guano. The cliffs of Drangey itself are a pandemonium of gulls, terns, guillemots, skuas, razorbills, and fulmars, while the tundra above is honeycombed with puffin burrows. As Eiríksson's boat drifts close, a cacophony of bird calls cascades down. If your mind dwells upon this noise, the mingled shrieks and peals begin to sound like a vast audience of people laughing hysterically. To be alone on Drangey for very long, you imagine, would drive you crazy.

Under the wear of wind and sea, the island's shape has changed significantly in the near-millennium since Grettir's day. Yet there is still only one landing place, on the island's west side. From there, a steep path winds through cliffs, across ledges, until, with the aid of heavy cable handrails and, at the top, a ladder, you emerge suddenly on the undulating green meadow that crowns this otherworldly retreat.

OVERLEAF: A BLACK PINNACLE CALLED THE KERLING ("CRONE"), COVERED WITH MURRES AND KÍTTIWAKES, FORMS A SATELLITE TO DRANGEY, WHOSE 570-FOOT CLIFFS LOOM BEHIND.

Eerie though Drangey is, Grettir and Illugi are happy there. They dine on birds, eggs, and mutton. Glaum climbs grumbling down to the shore every day to hunt for driftwood for the fire the hermits keep burning day and night. It is Glaum's job also to make sure he has pulled the top ladder up after him every night. Grettir makes a pet of a gray-bellied ram with huge horns, who follows the brothers wherever they go.

One day the farmers come out in a boat to gather their sheep for the slaughter. They are astounded to see men atop Drangey. Shouting from their boat, they converse with Grettir and learn that the famous outlaw has taken over their island. They offer to forget about the sheep Grettir has already slaughtered, if he will let them take the rest of their flock back to the mainland; they sweeten the offer with bribes. Grettir taunts them from his inviolate perch.

Thus begin years of scheming by the farmers and their allies to dislodge their unwanted tenant. Finally one man, Thorbjörn Ongul, buys out the others at bargain rates and vows to drive the great outlaw from Drangey. But after each fruitless expedition to the island, Thorbjörn rows home to the mockery of his neighbors.

One night Glaum lets the fire go out. "Grettir was furious," the saga tells us, "and said that Glaum deserved to be flogged. Glaum said he had a miserable life, staying there as an outlaw, and being beaten and abused whenever anything went wrong." Illugi urges sitting tight to wait for a passing boat, but Grettir decides to try to swim to the mainland. "He put on a tunic of homespun cloth which he tucked into his trousers; then the others made his fingers webbed." After a herculean swim, Grettir makes land at a hot spring called Reykir, bathes in it most of the night to shake off the chill, then crawls into the farmhouse and falls asleep. In the morning he recruits the farmer who had first rowed him to Drangey, and returns with fire to his brother and slave.

The distance from Drangey to Reykir (still a hot spring) is four miles, and the summer temperature of the seawater is 37–39° F. In homage to Grettir, and, implicitly, as a thumb-of-the-nose to all the fancy scholars who doubt the truth of the saga, during recent decades some of the best local swimmers have attempted to duplicate the outlaw's great swim. Five have made it.

There is no doubt in Eiríksson's mind that the saga tells the literal truth about Grettir. As you walk across the lovely summit meadow, he gives you a guided tour. This deep hollow in the turf, where the bedrock shows through, was Grettir's house: see how it keeps a lookout to the west, where Thorbjörn would approach. And this carved bowl in the bedrock—here Grettir kept his drinking water. The spring on which the three men depended, still the only source of fresh water on Drangey, lies under a gloomy overhang on the south cliff. To get to it today, you must go hand-over-hand down a knotted rope to a ledge, with a five-hundred-foot precipice beneath your feet—a jaunt Eiríksson, despite his years, performs casually.

The only regular visitors to Drangey nowadays are sportsmen who gather seabird eggs from the cliffs. A few years ago they built a small turf-roofed cabin on top. The process by which they go after the eggs is terrifying. Five or six men hold on to an inch-thick rope, the lower end of which is tied to the waist of the most intrepid member of the gang. They pass the rope over a kind of wooden pulley that is anchored at the edge of the cliff, then lower the

THOUSANDS OF BLACK-LEGGED KITTIWAKES NEST ON DRANGEY'S CLIFFS.

gatherer into the void. Wearing a baggy apron padded with grass, he dangles down among the screaming birds. The men above tie him off to a wooden stake pounded into the ground. Pushing with his feet, he makes himself swing sideways in a series of wild pendulums, deftly plucking eggs from nests as he flies past them. When his apron is full, his friends haul him bodily back to the top.

Like puffin-hunting, this ancient practice, which was once important for subsistence, is now pure sport. There are a few modern improvements. The men use walkie-talkies to communicate with the egg-gatherer, instead of simply leaning over the edge and shouting, as they used to. The wooden pulley is better than the old system, which was to lay the rope right on the rock edge, wrapping it in bulls'-hide to retard abrasion. (Eiríksson, who still goes down on the rope, points out the grooves in the cliff-edge worn by early lowerings.) Despite the protective sheath, ropes sometimes broke, sending the gatherer to his death.

Baring-Gould, who visited Drangey in 1862, was told that skuas were particularly dangerous antagonists, given to dive-bombing the egg-hunter. "The bird will descend with such velocity, that he has been known to impale himself on a spiked staff which the fowler holds in his hand." The Englishman went on to comment, "Drangey was said, in old times, to have been haunted by Trolls, who stretched out their arms from the hollows of the clefts as the fowler swung down, and clutching him, flung him to the bottom; but it is now believed that these Trolls were nothing more or less than Skuas." Amazingly enough, in Baring-Gould's time the fowlers seem simply to have held on to the thick horsehair rope rather than tying themselves to it.

LEFT: A FLEDGLING KITTIWAKE FLAPS ITS UNFEATHERED WINGS AT CLIFF'S EDGE NEAR THE SUMMIT OF DRANGEY. THE ONLY REGULAR VISITORS TO THE ISLAND TODAY ARE HUNTERS SEEKING BIRDS AND EGGS.

RIGHT: THE ONLY WAY TO REACH THE NORTH SUMMIT OF DRANGEY IS TO CLIMB AN OVERHANG OF ROTTEN ROCK. RUSTY CHAIN LINK LADDERS, PUT IN PLACE A GENERATION AGO BY DARING BIRD HUNTERS, SURMOUNT THE OVERHANG.

Meanwhile, in the saga, as Thorbjörn stews in his impotence, an athlete named Haering arrives from Norway: "he was young and so agile he could climb any cliff." Haering takes Drangey—and Grettir—as a personal challenge. Smuggled ashore, he attacks a route on the cliff that had never been climbed, while Thorbjörn distracts the brothers by bickering with them from his boat. With characteristic understatement, the saga tells what happens next:

> When [Haering] reached the top, he saw the brothers standing with their backs to him, so he thought that in a moment he would have won both fame and riches.... Then Illugi happened to glance in another direction, and he saw the man closing in on them.
>
> Illugi said, "Someone is coming up at us with a raised axe, and he seems to me rather unfriendly."
>
> "Why don't you turn and deal with him, then," said Grettir, "while I look after the ladder?"
>
> Illugi rushed at Haering, and the Easterner turned and ran away from him all round the island. Illugi chased him to the edge, and there Haering threw himself down over it, breaking every bone in his body, and killing himself. The place where he perished is still called Haering's Leap.

Eiríksson will gladly show you Haering's Leap. It is the southwest corner of the island, where the meadow narrows relentlessly to a sharp point. It is easy to imagine Illugi cornering the frantic Norwegian here.

Unable to capture Grettir by fair means, Thorbjörn resorts to the witchcraft of his aged foster-mother. Once more he rows out to Drangey, with the sorceress concealed under a pile of blankets. From hiding, she intones a

OVERLEAF: JÓN EIRÍKSSON GUIDES FRIENDS ON A TOUR OF DRANGEY'S SUMMIT. EIRÍKSSON CLAIMS THAT GRETTIR'S BONES LIE BURIED IN THE YARD OF HIS FARMSTEAD ON THE MAINLAND.

bitter curse on the outlaw. Deeply unsettled, Grettir says, "No other words have ever affected me as much as hers, and I know for certain that through her and her sorcery I shall suffer greatly. But she shall have something to remember her visit by." He picks up a rock and hurls it—a longer throw than men thought possible—and hits the witch, breaking her leg. (Eiríksson knows the exact spot from which Grettir threw his stone.)

Months later, the old woman asks Thorbjörn to take her in a cart down to the shore. There she finds a huge driftwood tree trunk, which she carves with runes, smears with her blood, and chants spells over. Thorbjörn pushes the trunk into the sea.

On two successive days, the brothers find the tree trunk, which has drifted ashore on Drangey. Illugi wants to save it for firewood, but Grettir kicks it back into the sea, suspecting evil. On the third day, hunting alone, Glaum scavenges the tree trunk and carries it up to the meadow. Failing to recognize the stump, Grettir swings his axe at it. The axe glances off and goes into his leg to the bone.

The wound festers, until Grettir is too weak to stand. Illugi is more vigilant than ever, but one day the disgruntled Glaum falls asleep, neglecting to pull up the top ladder. That night, under cover of darkness, Thorbjörn and eighteen allies reach Drangey. Startled to find the top ladder in place, they climb easily to the summit and attack the brothers in their house.

Illugi makes a heroic stand, but the warriors pull the house apart and capture him. Unable to defend himself, Grettir is already near death from his infected leg. But Thorbjörn and his men attack with a frenzy.

> They gave him many wounds, but there was little or no bleeding. When they thought that he must be dead, Thorbjörn grabbed at Grettir's short sword, and said that he had carried it long enough, but Grettir had locked his fingers so tightly around the hilt that Thorbjörn could not free it. Others went and tried; before they stopped, eight of them had tried to free it, but with no success.
>
> Then Thorbjörn said, "Why should we spare the outlaw? Put his hand on that beam."
>
> They did this, and Thorbjörn cut his hand off at the wrist; then the fingers straightened and let go of the hilt.

With Grettir's own short sword, Thorbjörn cuts off the outlaw's head.

In deference to his bravery and youth, Thorbjörn offers to spare Illugi's life if he swears never to take vengeance on the attackers. Illugi answers, "It is out of the question that I might save my life by becoming a coward like you. I will say only that no one will be a greater enemy of yours than I, if I live, for I will be slow to forget what you have done to Grettir. I would prefer to die." Thorbjörn's men execute Illugi on the spot.

On the eve of Grettir and Illugi's departure for their island refuge, years before, they had visited their mother in Bjarg to tell her their plans. In one of the most famous scenes in the sagas, she weeps bitterly and tells them, "Now you are going, my two sons, and you are fated to die together, and no one can escape the destiny that is shaped for him. I shall never again see either of you."

Atop a windswept hill near the farm at Bjarg, a monument to Grettir was raised in 1974. One of its four bronze bas-reliefs captures the mother's grief. But on the island where Iceland's greatest outlaw met his end, there is no memorial—unless it be the wave-lashed grandeur of Drangey itself.

A CLIMBER ASCENDS THE LADDER TO DRANGEY'S NORTH SUMMIT.

OVERLEAF: DRANGEY, THE CLIFF-GIRDED ISLAND IN THE NORTH THAT BECAME GRETTIR'S FINAL REFUGE, IS SEEN HERE SHORTLY AFTER MIDNIGHT IN JULY.

IN THE WESTFJORDS, FOGGY
UPLAND MOORS SEPARATE
DEEPLY INDENTED BAYS. OLD
FOOTPATHS MARKED WITH
GIANT CAIRNS CROSS THESE
DESOLATE MOORS FROM
TOWN TO TOWN.

# OUTLAWS
# AND
# CHRISTIANS

THE WESTFJORDS IS THE NAME OF THE LARGE PENINSULA that thrusts toward Greenland at the northwest corner of Iceland. Here are the deepest and most spectacular inlets in the country, the most tortured coastline, and some of the loneliest moorlands. The whole of the Westfjords is prevented from being a separate island only by a five-mile-wide neck of land between the Gilsfjörður and the Bitrufjörður, which attaches it to the rest of Iceland. Although settled early, this was one of the last inhabited regions to have roads, which even today are rough and unpaved.

Auden thought this "the most beautiful and the least visited part of Iceland." For eleven centuries, the jagged shores of the Westfjords have caused more than their share of shipwrecks. As you stand on some cliff a thousand feet above the ocean, you will see, on the rocky coast below, far from any road, a minuscule orange dot. This is a *neyðarskýli*, or emergency shelter. A squat wooden box, it typically contains only a blanket or two, a little canned food, and perhaps a gas stove, but such refuges have saved the lives of many shipwrecked sailors and stranded travelers over the years.

These orange huts are also found on the broad summits of the moors. Because the coast is so hard to walk, the early settlers of the seaport towns, long before there were any roads, made paths across the treeless heaths that separate one fjord from another. They marked these paths with cairns at intervals, many of which still stand. Only these man-high piles of rock kept travelers from becoming lost in the thick fogs so prevalent on the moors.

The Westfjords divide into three main branches, stretching west, north-west, and north from the neck of the peninsula. The northern branch is one of the scenically most splendid parts of Iceland. A small glacier called the Drangajökull sprawls in the center of this wilderness; to the south the moors are sprinkled with tiny lakes; on the north coast, the Hornstrandir, parabolic sweeps of meadow-hung precipice, shelter huge colonies of seabirds. In summer the whole sub-peninsula is a riot of wildflowers.

Yet this branch of the Westfjords has a harsh climate: it is the last coast in the country to see the winter snows melt. Although many people once lived here, the region has been slowly depopulated during this century: a diagonal line marking the northern limit of habitation has crept steadily southward over the decades. On a fine summer day, you can stop your car on coastal highway 61 and stare over the Ísafjarðardjúp, to see, glittering in the sun, once-prosperous farmhouses across the bay that now stand empty. Everywhere else in Iceland the population is either expanding or holding its own; here is the only place that is being systematically abandoned.

In 1897 Collingwood sailed past the Hornstrandir, glimpsing the poor huts of the natives, whom he memorialized in a somber paragraph:

> Along this inhospitable coast live the least known and most forlorn of Icelanders. They are cut off from communication with the rest of the world for a great part of the year. They have to wait for weeks or months in winter before they can get to church to be baptized or married, or to bury their dead. Once, the story goes, they left a coffin in the snow, being overtaken by a storm on their way to church. All winter they had to leave it there. When spring came, the melting of the snowdrifts at last uncovered the body, and the funeral so strangely interrupted could be accomplished. Many a tourist has passed the Hornstrandir on his steamboat voyage; but very few strangers have ever set foot on the coast or made the acquaintance of its people, the most primitive of all the inhabitants of Iceland.

The Westfjords is the setting for one of the most sharply tragic of the sagas. *The Saga of Gísli* is an emotionally fraught tale full of secrets, betrayals, overheard confessions, and sensual enticements in the night. Its hero, Gísli Súrsson, is trapped by fate in an impossible predicament: to avenge the murder of his best friend, who is also his wife's brother, he must kill his sister's husband. The scene in which Gísli steals into his sister's bedroom in the dark to perform this deed, carrying his matchless spear, Greyflank, is one of the most disturbing in the sagas, mingling the intimate and incestuous with the sanguinary:*

> Now he goes farther into the room to the bed closet where Thorgrím slept, and his sister, and the door was ajar, and they are both in bed. He goes up and gropes about inside and puts his hand on his sister's breast; she was sleeping next the outside.
>
> Then Thórdís spoke. "Why is your hand so cold, Thorgrím?" and she wakes him.
>
> Thorgrím asked: "Do you want me to turn your way?" She thought he had put his arm over her.
>
> Gísli waits yet for a while, and warms his hand in his shirt, and they both go to sleep; then he takes hold of Thorgrím gently, so that he wakes up. He thought that Thórdís had roused him, and he turned to her. Gísli pulls back the covers with one

---

*This translation, by George Johnston, is one of the few that renders in English a peculiarity of the style of the sagas, namely the frequent alternation of past and present tenses.

AT THE NORTH CAPE OF THE CENTRAL BRANCH OF THE WESTFJORDS, THE TWO-THOUSAND-FOOT CLIFFS OF THE STIGAHLIÐ PLUNGE TOWARD THE SEA.

hand, and with the other he thrusts Greyflank into Thorgrím so that it goes through him and sticks in the bed.

Gísli flees before his sister can recognize him, but eventually his identity as the murderer is discovered. He becomes an outlaw—the second most famous in Iceland. As the saga itself editorializes, "It is agreed among all wise men that Gísli went longer as an outlaw than any other man, except Grettir Asmundsson." Most reckonings give Grettir's tenure at large as nineteen years, Gísli's as fourteen.

As you travel across the moors of the Westfjords today, it is easy to imagine how a fugitive could hide among the wrinkled cliffs and plunging valleys. After his outlawry, Gísli's faithful wife Aud lives alone at her farm at the head of the Geirthjófsfjörður. His enemies suspect Aud of harboring Gísli, and they are right, but for years they search the valley fruitlessly because the outlaw has found a perfect hiding place among cliffs above the farmstead.

From his dreams, however, Gísli cannot hide. He is haunted by a pair of dream women, one good, one bad, both seeming to prophesy his future. The good woman shows him kinsmen before a fireplace and a rich house full of cushioned benches. The bad woman, however, comes to him more and more often, tying a bloody cap on his head, then washing his head in blood. Soon, like Grettir, Gísli is afraid to be alone in the dark.

Inevitably, one day his enemies find him, having tracked his footsteps in the first frost of winter to his secret hiding place. They come fifteen strong to kill the great outlaw.

The cliff where Gísli died, called Einhamar, lies far from any road today. At

LEFT: NEAR LÁTRABJARG IN THE WESTFJORDS, THE REMAINS OF AN OLD FISHING STATION LIE SMOTHERED IN THE GRASS.

CENTER: A WRECKED FISHING BOAT LIES BEACHED IN THE WESTFJORDS.

RIGHT: AN OLD HULL ROTS ON THE JETTY AT ISAFJÖRÐUR, LARGEST TOWN IN THE WESTFJORDS AND ONE OF THE OLDEST TRADING CENTERS IN ICELAND.

the head of the Geirthjófsfjörður, which is reached only by boat, a lone farm-house stands exactly where Aud's did a millennium before. A thousand feet above, crossing the bleak moor called the Dynjandiheiði, Highway 60, a mere dirt track, links a pair of small towns sixty miles apart. Few people take the trouble to hike from the road down the nameless stream to find Gísli's hide-out and Einhamar, but the pilgrimage is worth the effort.

There is no trail. As the tundra slopes from summer snowbanks down toward the cliffs that guard the stream, thickets of willow block the way. You must bushwhack through these to find the cataracts among which Gísli hid for fourteen years, then wade the numbing stream to approach Einhamar. On this otherwise nondescript cliff, someone in 1930 carved an exquisite bas-relief memorial to Gísli. The oval design is lettered around the border; at the top, a shield covers a crossed halberd and spear; at the bottom, a snake coils across the margin of the inscription. Sixty years' growth of lichen on the granite slab have dimmed the carving, giving it a gray patina.

From a ledge atop this slab, if tradition bears the truth, Gísli made what Icelanders regard as the bravest stand of any doomed hero. Pierced with spears, assaulted from two sides, Gísli fights on. By the time he is done, eight of his enemy lie dead. As the saga relates:"They attack him fiercely, Eyjólf and his kinsmen; they saw that their honor was at stake. They wound him then with their spears, so that his bowels begin to come out; and he gathers the bowels in with his shirt and ties them underneath with the cord. Then Gísli told them to wait a little—'You will finish up the case as you want to.' He spoke a verse:"

Sheer goddess of shower
Of spear-shaft's hall, cheer-heart,
Brave, bids of her lover,
Bold one, the cold tidings.
Fain am I though finely
Forged bright edges bite me;
My sire's true sword temper,
Shows in his son's life-close.

Having spoken the last line, Gísli buries his sword in the skull of a last antagonist, leaps from the cliff, and dies.

Gísli's is, in the world of the sagas, the perfect death for a hero—to fight against impossible odds, to treat one's mortal wounds with sangfroid, then to perish with a polished scaldic verse on one's lips. For our modern taste, it may seem all too cavalier, as idealized and improbable as a gunslinger's death in a western movie.

To anyone who reads widely in the sagas, an obvious but important question occurs: was Iceland in the tenth century really as bloody as these tales imply? Was it a place in which the slightest insults regularly provoked murder? Apologists for the country argue that the preponderance of feud and killing in the sagas greatly exaggerates reality: along with these occasional battles to the death, the early generations must have been full of unspectacular farming, fishing, childbearing, and neighborliness.

This contention is certainly just. We would get a warped view of Greek life if we knew it only from the *Iliad* and the *Odyssey*—or of the Old West from Clint Eastwood movies alone. Men like Gísli, Grettir, and Gunnar are by definition exceptional, as are their fates. (Achilles was not a typical Athenian, nor Billy the Kid an average citizen of New Mexico in the 1870s.)

The sagas are little influenced by the conventions of medieval European romance. There is almost none of the formalized pageantry of battle that we get in Chaucer's *The Knight's Tale* or the *Chanson de Roland*. Yet the hand-to-hand frays in the sagas depend on stylized conventions of their own, hinting at literary effects that supersede verisimilitude. One of the standard feats that great heroes such as Gunnar perform is to catch a thrown spear in midair and hurl it back, piercing the antagonist who launched it. Heads and limbs are lopped cleanly off with a single swing of a keen-edged halberd or sword. A well-thrust spear pierces both shield and body, killing in a stroke. Grettir's death is all the more ignominious in that the fatal blow comes from his own redoubtable short sword. Often in the sagas men name the weapons that have been given them by kings or other great warriors and believe that luck in battle depends on their retaining possession: Gísli with his spear Greyflank; Thorgeir, one of Njál's avengers, with his axe Battle-Troll; Bolli and his sword Leg-Biter in the *Laxdaela Saga*.

Some of the feats performed by heroes in battle defy credibility. Flosi's leap at the Althing was certainly the greatest long jump in medieval Iceland. Grettir's stoning the witch in the boat with one throw from hundreds of feet above was remarkable enough, but we are asked to believe that, during the Burning, Skarp-Heðin, one of Njál's sons, could have taken a tooth that he kept in a bag, a souvenir from the skull of a former victim, and thrown it at one of the burners with such force and accuracy that "the eye was gouged from its socket onto the cheek." These deeds are presented not as marvels

performed with the aid of supernatural powers, but as the sort of exceptional feats heroes summon up in crises.

The near-absurd stylization of battle can be seen in a classic episode such as the one in which Skarp-Heðin harvests the tooth. With four friends, he is crossing the Markar River on an ice floe when eight opponents confront him.

> Skarp-Heðin made a leap and cleared the channel between the ice-banks, steadied himself, and at once went into a slide: the ice was glassy-smooth, and he skimmed along as fast as a bird.
>
> Thrain was then about to put on his helmet. Skarp-Heðin came swooping down on him and swung at him with his axe. The axe crashed down on his head and split it down to the jaw-bone, spilling the back-teeth on to the ice. It all happened so quickly that no one had time to land a blow on Skarp-Heðin as he skimmed past at great speed. Tjorvi threw a shield into his path, but Skarp-Heðin cleared it with a jump without losing his balance and slid to the other end of the sheet-ice.

If such a prodigy was based on any historical deed at all, we can imagine it so revised in the telling over the three hundred years between the event and its recording in the saga that it takes on the economy of legend.

To die well is the ultimate accomplishment, as the siege at Einhamar shows. (At the turn of the century, when the sagas were still widely read by Icelandic adolescents, Gísli was the great heartthrob for girls.) If a warrior could not manufacture a scaldic verse with his dying breath, a nonchalant witticism was next best. Some of these last lines have a morbid humor about them—an intentional effect. At the onset of the ambush of Gunnar at Hliðarendi, Thorgrím climbs onto the roof to see if the hero is at home; Gunnar plants his halberd in Thorgrím's belly, making him fall off the roof.

> He strode over to where Gizur and the others were sitting.
>
> Gizur looked up at him and asked, "Is Gunnar at home?"
>
> "That's for you to find out," replied Thorgrím. "But I know that his halberd certainly is."
>
> And with that he fell dead.

Having been treacherously speared through the body, Atli in *Grettir's Saga* utters a bemused last sentence: "Broad spears are becoming fashionable nowadays." In *Njál's Saga*, Killer-Hrapp seems to have some sense of his moral standing. When Helgi cuts off his arm, he says, "What you have done certainly needed doing; that hand has brought harm and death to many." A moment later he lies dead.

There is something like chivalry in operation here, or at least a code of what we might call Viking machismo. Not all deaths in the sagas are clean or heroic, however, and some of the more grisly passages reveal an occasional resort to torture. When Hrafnkel and his men get their comeuppance in *Hrafnkel's Saga*, they have holes cut through their heels behind the tendons and a rope strung through, and are then hung upside down from a clothes' beam. In *Njál's Saga* the malefactor Broðir is treated even more cruelly. "Úlf Hreða slit open his belly and unwound his intestines from his stomach by leading him round and round an oak tree; and Broðir did not die before they had all been pulled out of him." All such demises are narrated in the sagas in a cool, neutral tone. There is little room for pity or remorse.

SEEN FROM THE SUMMIT OF SANDAFELL IN THE WESTFJORDS, A FILE OF UNNAMED MOUNTAINS RANGES TO THE SOUTH: THIS IS THE COUNTRY OF GÍSLI'S SAGA.

OVERLEAF: RAYS OF SUN PIERCE CLOUD COVER ON THE DYRAFJÖRÐUR, THE BAY WHERE GÍSLI'S ENEMIES SAILED TO HUNT HIM DOWN.

One of the most mysterious yet recurrent figures in the sagas is the berserker. These were warriors who went into trances during which they fought maniacally, indifferent to pain, capable of superhuman strength. (The Icelandic word literally means "bear-shirted.") Such men are greatly prized as warriors, but feared the rest of the time on account of their violent and erratic nature. It is even considered kosher to double-cross them. A classic instance occurs in the *Eyrbyggja Saga*. Two berserkers, Swedish brothers named Halli and Leiknir, come to Iceland, where Halli falls in love with the daughter of a chieftain named Styr. Halli proposes that he and his brother will give steadfast support to Styr in exchange for his daughter's hand. Styr sets a great labor as a test of their worthiness: they are to clear a pathway across the lava field that abuts Styr's farm. Halli and Leiknir succeed in this monumental work. When they are done, Styr invites them to relax in a steam bath he has built. Once the Swedes are inside, he piles rocks on the door, pours scalding water in, and spears the berserkers as they try to escape. (The Berserkjahraun, or Berserkers' Lava, sprawls along the north coast of Snae-fellsnes. According to the *Iceland Road Guide*, portions of Halli and Leiknir's path are still visible, as well as their burial mound.)

Modern commentators have wondered whether in the berserker the sagas may describe a medical condition—either extreme paranoia, or manic-depressive illness, or epileptic seizures, or lycanthropy, the delusion of being transformed into a wild beast. It may be, however, that the berserker is as much a literary convention as the spear caught in midflight.

Although the sagas abound in the supernatural, it is striking that the gods play almost no part in their action. Instead, an overarching Fate seems to rule the sublunary world. The medieval Icelander accepts without demurral the notion that things are preordained. It is as Grettir's mother says, already mourning her sons before they leave for Drangey, "No one can escape the destiny that is shaped for him." With his second sight, Njál foresees the death of his family, but he is powerless to prevent it. At the Althing, shortly before the Burning, Snorri Goði tells Skarp-Heðin, on first meeting him, "I think you look very ruthless and formidable, but my guess is that you have exhausted your store of good luck, and that you have not long to live." "Well and good," answers the son of Njál, "for death is a debt we all have to pay."

This notion of Fate helps account for the extraordinary bravery saga heroes display. Yet Fate, like the gods, operates in quixotic and devious ways. The sagas sometimes pivot, in moments of high drama, on trivial events. The errant shoe-thong crops up with the regularity of a literary convention: rush-ing into battle or fleeing an enemy, a man breaks his shoe-thong or trips on his shoelace and thus determines the outcome of his life. In the Burning, the agent of Fate is a pile of chickweed kept behind the house. One day an apparently senile old woman starts pounding the chickweed with a cudgel.

> Skarp-Heðin laughed at this, and asked her why she was so angry with the chick-weed.
>
> The old woman replied, "This chickweed will be used as the kindling when they burn Njál and my foster-child Bergthóra [Njáls' wife] inside the house. Quick, take it away and throw it into some water or burn it."
>
> "No," said Skarp-Heðin, "for if that is what is ordained, something else will be found to kindle the fire even if this chickweed is not here."

The chickweed, of course, is used just as the old woman predicts.

Though entirely consonant with Norse mythology, the idea of an ineluctable destiny took hold with a special tenacity in medieval Iceland. Christianity preached its own version of predestination, but Viking Fate was one of the beliefs it sought most diligently to eradicate. And with little success: according to Magnússon, among present-day Icelanders, "The notion of predestination is very much alive. One does what one is fated to do, and dies at a preordained moment....The notion is especially deep-rooted among seamen and those who work at dangerous occupations."

Given the philosophical temper of early Iceland, it is remarkable that Christianity could make any inroads at all, let alone that the country would officially adopt the religion after only four generations of settlement. Such a change did not come easily; in fact, the issue of religion threatened to turn a fragile nation-in-the-making toward all-out civil war.

There were a few Christians such as Helgi the Lean among the early settlers, but their beliefs had little impact on their neighbors; some, in fact, reverted to paganism. It was not until 981 that Iceland saw its first Christian missionary. He was an Icelander of noble birth named Thorvald, who traveled much abroad, was converted in Germany, and returned to Iceland with fire in his eyes. He crisscrossed the country making converts, but so alienated his compatriots that the Althing outlawed him after five years. Thorvald ended up as a recluse in a Russian monastery.

 Other missionaries followed. "Most of them were Thorvald's inferiors," says Magnússon; "some of them outright bandits." The *Laxdaela Saga* gives us a glimpse of one. "Thangbrand brought his ship to Alptafjord, and stayed the winter with Hall of Siða at Thvattriver, where he preached the faith with bland words and harsh measures; he killed the two men who opposed him most." By far the most important factor in Christianizing Iceland, however, was that King Óláf Tryggvason of Norway, who reigned from 995 to 1000, had become a fanatical Christian bent on converting all the Norse-speaking countries.

In the *Laxdaela Saga*, which was written by a Christian in the thirteenth century, and which, of all the major sagas, may be the one most influenced by Christian ideas and style, there is a striking scene in which the hero Kjartan Óláfsson, traveling in Norway, gets caught up in a local swimming contest.

> Kjartan now plunged into the river and made for this man who was the best swimmer, and forced him under water at once and held him there for a while before letting go of him. No sooner had they come to the surface than this man seized hold of Kjartan and pulled him down, and they stayed under for what seemed to Kjartan a very reasonable time. They surfaced for a second time, and still they exchanged no words. Then they went under for a third time and now they stayed down much longer than before. Kjartan was no longer sure how this game would end, and felt that he had never been in such a tight corner before. At last they came to the surface and swam ashore.

His opponent compliments Kjartan and asks him his name, then says, "Why don't you ask anything about me?"

> "I don't care what your name is," said Kjartan.
>   The townsman said, "You are not only highly accomplished but you are arrogant as well. But you shall know my name nevertheless, and against whom you have been swimming. I am King Óláf Tryggvason."

Initially surly, Kjartan is at last persuaded to attend a church to investigate for himself the strange religion. He becomes one of Óláf's prize converts.

This account in the saga, with its overtones of baptism, its structure as Christian homily, is historically dubious. It gives, however, a lively picture of the struggle for minds and hearts between the old and new faiths in Iceland as the first millennium closed.

With greater historical certainty, we know that the question of religion reached a crisis at the Althing in the year 1000. The hotheads in each camp wanted to settle the issue with arms. Many Christians urged seceding from the heathens and establishing their own state, with a separate government. Either course would have been disastrous for Iceland's future. One of the best (and earliest) accounts of what happened instead is in *Njál's Saga*.

> The Christians chose Hall of Siða to be their Law-Speaker; but Hall went to see Thorgeir the Priest of Ljósawater, and gave him three marks of silver to proclaim what the law should be. It was taking a risk, for Thorgeir was a heathen.
>
> For a whole day, Thorgeir lay with a cloak over his head. No one spoke to him. Next day, people gathered at the Law Rock.
>
> Thorgeir asked to be heard, and said, "It seems to me that an impossible situation arises if we do not all have one and the same law. If the laws are divided the peace will be divided, and we cannot tolerate that. Now, therefore, I want to ask heathens and Christians whether they will accept the law which I am going to proclaim."
>
> They all agreed. Thorgeir insisted on oaths and binding pledges from them; they all agreed to that, and gave him their pledge.
>
> "The first principle of our laws," declared Thorgeir, "is that all men in this land shall be Christian and believe in the one God—Father, Son, and Holy Ghost—and renounce all worship of idols. They shall not expose children at birth nor eat horseflesh. The penalty for carrying on these practices openly shall be outlawry, but they shall not be punishable if they are done in private." . . .
>
> The heathens felt they had been grossly betrayed, but despite that the new faith became law, and the whole land became Christian.

If this is indeed what transpired at the Althing that climactic June in the year 1000, then Thorgeir was one of the great diplomatic strategists in history. It was very canny of him, for instance, to appeal to the Viking sense of honor by making the chieftains pledge their obedience *before* he announced his decision. In one stroke both civil war and secession were averted. The country became irrevocably Christian, and the next two centuries were more peaceful on the whole than the turbulent times that had preceded them.

Among the most important consequences of the Christianizing of Iceland was the rise of a written literature. The excellence of the sagas as we know them—not to mention the power of the *Edda* and other poems, or the value of the histories, commentaries, and law codes that have come down to us— depended on Iceland's developing a climate of Christian learning.

Yet in most respects, the country did not change radically in the year 1000. The pagan values lived on, as the sagas, written as late as the fourteenth century, abundantly demonstrate. To be sure, there are Christian elements through and through these prose works. As Njál resigns himself to death during the Burning, for instance, he says to the terrified women in his household, "Be of good heart and speak no words of fear, for this is just a passing storm and it will be long before another like it comes. Put your faith in the mercy of God, for He will not let us burn both in this world and the next."

BREIÐAVÍK CHURCH IN THE WESTFJORDS: A REMARKABLE NUMBER OF ICELAND'S CHURCHES STAND IN THE MIDST OF WHAT SEEMS ALL-BUT-UNINHABITED COUNTRY, YET THEIR PARISHIONERS ASSEMBLE EVERY SUNDAY.

OVERLEAF: AN ISOLATED FARMSTEAD NESTLES UNDER THE CLIFF NEAR THE CASCADE OF SELJALANDSFOSS.

In a work such as the Anglo-Saxon *Beowulf*, it is the scholar's job to try to separate the pagan heart of the poem from the Christian "adulterations" that have been grafted onto it by later writers. Such platitudes as Njál's, however, do not create a similar problem. All during the last half of the Saga Age, the debate over faith occupied Iceland. The saga itself tells us that Njál was converted by Thangbrand, the missionary of "bland words and harsh measures," more than a decade before his death. During the Burning, he may well have uttered pieties such as the one the saga puts in his mouth. The great wonder of the sagas—and a concomitant of their glory—is that there is so little of Christian thought and art in them.

The first church in Iceland was built in Thingvellir in 1018. In 1056 an Icelandic bishopric was established at Skálholt, on an isolated riverbank in the southwest; fifty years later a second was added at Hólar in the north. The early churches of Iceland, built mainly of wood, have survived no better than the houses. What little we know of the cathedrals at Skálholt and Hólar only whets the imagination. They measured a rambling 200 feet by 35 feet and stood 40 feet high—probably the largest wooden churches ever built in medieval Scandinavia. They were, moreover, monuments of Romanesque style. To build a church in wood on such a grand scale was so rare for the period that an architectural historian would give his eyeteeth to see such a cathedral still standing.

In 1897, Collingwood found only a "bare wooden shanty" where the cathedral had been at Skálholt. Under the floor, however, he discovered marble

LEFT: TURNHUS FARM AT ISAFJÖÐUR, BUILT IN 1785, REMAINS AS ONE OF THE FEW EXISTING BUILDINGS OF ITS TYPE FROM THAT DATE.

CENTER: A NICELY MOLDED WOODEN WINDOW PUNCTUATES THE DRAB PATTERN OF AN UNPAINTED WALL OF CORRUGATED IRON IN AN ISAFJÖRÐUR HOUSE.

RIGHT: THE SMALL LUTHERAN CHURCHES SCATTERED ACROSS THE COUNTRYSIDE ARE ICELAND'S LOVELIEST HUMAN ORNAMENT. THE CHURCH AT GRUND, NEAR AKUREYRI, STANDS ON THE SITE OF ONE OF THE MOST IMPORTANT FOURTEENTH-CENTURY FARMSTEADS.

slabs that had evidently been carved in Italy and even earlier stones lying "broken and defaced beneath the timbers," the last remnants of the cathedral. Today not even these stones remain: a handsome modern church stands at Skálholt, but the site is lonelier than ever, neglected by tourists and Icelanders alike. Collingwood was scandalized to witness, all over the country, the indifference with which old churches and their unique relics were treated. "There is little feeling in Iceland for such things," he wrote. "The clergy build their houses with broken bits of their predecessors' tombs, or lay the sculptured stone down for path flags."

In the sixteenth century the Reformation hit Iceland with a sudden violence. The last bishop at Skálholt was beheaded. Iceland became Lutheran in a matter of a few decades. Lutheran it remains today, with ninety-seven percent of the populace belonging to the church, although Christian faith may by now be largely pro forma. A recent survey produced the paradoxical result that while ninety-seven percent of Icelanders consider themselves at least somewhat religious, ninety-two percent never read the Bible.

Yet the countryside all over Iceland is dotted with small Lutheran churches, which are its loveliest human ornament. There is a church in every village, but the most striking sit alone on the margin of a windswept fjord or beneath some frowning precipice. Where do their parishioners come from? There are hundreds of such isolated churches, even in the most benighted landscapes; they seem to sew the country together, to promise a communal life where there might otherwise be only gloom and toil.

Icelandic churches are a colorful lot, unlike the country's farmhouses, for which the commonest hues are a pale cream for the walls, a dull salmon for the roof. The churches observe no such regularity, although pastel is de rigueur. They are painted in the subtlest shades—the green of old hay, the russet of ripening apples, a chalky purple with brown in it, a blue weighted with lead. Nor do the churches fall into any single design, though they keep to certain conventions. The belfry is normally square, steep, and brimmed like a hat; sometimes an octagonal lantern tower takes its place, and in some modern churches soaring shafts lengthen the belfries—but always the effect is decorous. The windows are plain, stained glass being a rarity in Iceland. The body of the church is square and solid, the east facade flat and unpretentious. You wander close, admiring, open the gate to the grassy cemetery that surrounds the church, and walk through it toward the door. The surprise comes all at once: the outside of the church is not wood, as you had assumed from afar, but corrugated iron. The very stuff that makes the towns so drab and utilitarian is here somehow tamed into art.

Inside, there are a bare nave, a few rows of wooden benches, and a clean Protestant light coming through the windows. The altarpiece, usually a *Last Supper*, was rendered perhaps by a naive Icelandic painter who set a scrawny-looking chicken on the table for Christ's meal. The hymnal tunes look plodding on the page. The mysteries that obsessed medieval Europe, of a God who died tortured by those he meant to save, to be refleshed in the mouths of the faithful as bread and wine, have a dim, abstract relevance here. But the windows call you back outside, where the endless landscape, the most real thing in Iceland, beckons.

THE CHURCH AT VALLANES GUARDS THE SHORE OF THE LONG LAKE CALLED THE LÖGURINN.

OVERLEAF: AN ELEGANT MODERNISM UPDATES THE TRADITIONAL FORMULA FOR ECCLESIASTICAL ARCHITECTURE AT SAURBAER ON THE HVALFJÖRÐUR.

A WINTER-STRUCK CHURCH
STANDS ON THE OUTER
SNAEFELLSNES PENINSULA.

# WOMEN
# AND
# WINTER

WITH THEIR GRIM BATTLES AND IDEAL DEATHS, THEIR bouts of ale-drinking and bursts of scaldic eloquence, their wranglings at the Althing and wanderings through the wilderness, the sagas seem to postulate a world thoroughly dominated by men. What, within this world, was the place of women?

In the sagas, women are never placed on pedestals. There is no trace in Iceland of the romantic European tradition of haughty princesses for whose favor knights joust in tournaments, of modest virgins whose graces troubadors catalogue in their lays. There is, in fact, almost nothing in the sagas that resembles a sustained love story. Women are treated with the same blunt realism that delineates a horsefight or a ball game on the ice. Virginity is unimportant.

The saga world, like every other medieval European society of which we know, was indeed dominated by men. But the tellers of the Icelandic tales neither ignore women, nor, on the whole, condescend to them. In many important actions women play pivotal roles. Thus, for example, in the *Laxdaela Saga*, the quarreling half-brothers Hrút and Hoskuld are about to strap on their weapons for a battle to the death when Jorunn, Hoskuld's wife, intercedes by pouring vigorous scorn into her husband's ear. Her speech, which is given in full in the saga, is rich in wisdom. It persuades Hoskuld to reconsider, and he is lastingly reconciled with Hrút.

In the eerie murder scene in *Gísli's Saga*, it will be recalled, Gísli's sister Thórdís lies in bed with her husband when Gísli runs the man through with

his spear. She is later forced to marry Bork, one of the men who hunts Gísli down. The *Eyrbyggja Saga* gives us a sequel to Thórdís's story after her brother's death. Eyjólf, who led the assault on Einhamar where the great outlaw fell, comes to visit Bork, bragging of his conquest. Bork demands that his wife serve a meal to Eyjólf. As she lays a bowl of porridge before her brother's killer, Thórdís drops a spoon. Bending over beneath the table, she seizes Eyjólf's own sword and gives him a deep wound to the thigh. Bork strikes his wife, but another man steps between them to save her.

Shortly thereafter Bork decides to move his home. His wife surprises him with what may seem a very modern act: "Thórdís stepped forward and named witnesses to the fact that she declared herself divorced from her husband Bork, and gave as grounds the fact that he had struck her; and she declared she would never again endure his blows. Then the property of both was divided...."

As this passage suggests, women in Iceland enjoyed considerable rights before the law. Some of the pioneer settlers were women, such as Unn the Deep-Minded, whose courage at sea, leadership abilities, wisdom as a land-holder, and noble death are applauded in the *Laxdaela Saga*. Women in Iceland had completely equal connubial rights, and could declare themselves divorced, as Thórdís does, on grounds ranging from incompatibility to non-consummation of marriage. So far from the troubador tradition were Icelandic mores, that it was actually against the law to compose love songs to a woman, for fear this might compromise her marital prospects. In general, marriages were arranged, insofar as an enterprising young man would propose to the father of a woman he and his kinsfolk saw as improving his standing; the woman's consent, however, usually had to be obtained. No other European country at the time offered women anything like these privileges.

The sagas, it is true, display a classic male ambivalence about feminine virtues and faults. Sometimes women are implicitly praised for being as ruthless and coldhearted as warriors. One such is Thuríd in the *Laxdaela Saga*, who trades her baby for the sword Leg-Biter. Hallgerd, the proud beauty of *Njál's Saga*, on being told by his killer of the death of her beloved second husband, only laughs and says, "There's nothing halfhearted about your way of doing things." She then tricks the man into seeking refuge with her uncle, who she knows will slay him. In this cool, efficient manner, she avenges her husband.

Women in the sagas act with brave independence. They harbor outlaws, serve as spies, choose lovers from among their suitors. On the other hand, it is mainly women who are accused of witchcraft. In the *Eyrbyggja Saga*, a woman named Geirríd and a man named Gunnlaug seem to be courting. One night Geirríd asks him to stay over rather than walk home, for she fears that "water witches are about." Gunnlaug declines and sets off in the darkness. He is found unconscious: "He was all black and blue about the shoulders, and the flesh was torn from his bones." Geirríd is accused of being a "night hag" and of having "ridden" Gunnlaug, and is brought to trial. She is, however, acquitted.

The sagas reserve a special revulsion for that dangerous creature, the she-troll, whom heroes must hunt down in their cave lairs and fight to the death. These "ogresses" tend to be huge, filthy, silent, and inhumanly strong.

Since romantic love plays so little part in the sagas, sexuality is rarely

FOR CENTURIES, POETS AND TRAVELERS HAVE SUNG THE BEAUTY OF ICELANDIC WOMEN: HILDUR DUNGAL WAS A FINALIST IN THE 1989 MISS ICELAND CONTEST.

OVERLEAF: UPRIGHT BASALT COLUMNS FROM THE CLIFF AT GERÐUBERG ON SNAEFELLSNES.

131

sublimated to its service, as it so often is in continental romance. Instead, sex often takes on a homely, comic aura; the saga writer treats it with a bawdy forthrightness not much different in tone from Chaucer's or Boccaccio's. In *Njál's Saga*, Hrút, a great warrior from Iceland in attendance at King Harald Grey-Cloak's court in Norway, is taken under the wing of the aging queen mother, Gunnhild. He is betrothed back home to the lovely Unn, but when Gunnhild orders him to her bed, he does not disobey. The homesick Hrút finally begs to return to Iceland. Gunnhild gives him a gold bracelet, kisses him goodbye, and leaves a curse: "The spell I now lay on you will prevent your ever enjoying the woman in Iceland on whom you have set your heart. With other women you may have your will, but never with her."

Curses in the sagas always take effect: Hrút and Unn are unable to make love. Unn comes to her father to complain; he asks her to be more explicit. In the rather circumlocutory phrasing of the English translation, she says, "Whenever he touches me, he is so enlarged that he cannot have enjoyment of me, although we both passionately desire to reach consummation. But we have never succeeded. And yet, before we draw apart, he proves that he is by nature as normal as other men." Unn divorces Hrút on the grounds that their marriage cannot be consummated. This contretemps is handled not as a tragedy, but as a mere turn of bad luck. Unn and Hrút separate and go on with their lives.

In *Grettir's Saga*, after the hero has swum to Reykir to bring fire back to Drangey and has collapsed of exhaustion in the farmhouse, two young women find him lying naked on the floor. "He is certainly big enough in the

LEFT: A RUNESTONE LIES ATOP THE GRAVE OF SKALLAGRÍM KVELDÚLFSSON AT BORGARNES. DURING THE FIRST TWO CENTURIES OF CIVILIZATION, ICELAND HAD NO TRUE WRITTEN LANGUAGE AND ONLY A HANDFUL OF RUNESTONES FROM THOSE YEARS SURVIVE.

RIGHT: ON THE SITE OF THE THÓRSNES-THING, ONE OF TWO ICELANDIC ASSEMBLIES THAT PREDATED THE ALTHING, HALLI, A BOY FROM THE LOCAL FARM, PLAYS WITH HIS DOG.

chest," giggles the maid, "but it seems to me very odd how small he is farther down. That part of him isn't up to the rest of him." Grettir overhears the maid, seizes her, pulls her onto a bench, and utters a scaldic boast:

> The wench has complained
> that my penis is small,
> and the boastful slut
> may well be right.
> But a small one can grow,
> and I'm still a young man,
> so wait until I get
> into action, my lass.

The euphemistic translation implies a rape: "The maid kept crying out, but in the end, before they parted, she had stopped taunting him."

Although apparently uninterested in marriage, Grettir takes carnal pleasures as his due. During one of his fugitive residencies, in a mountain valley ruled by a giant half-troll named Thórir, Grettir "said that he had a good deal of fun with Thórir's daughters, and that they liked it too, for there were not many visitors around." One of Grettir's poems was so licentious that an early owner of the only manuscript in which it was preserved erased it. With ultraviolet light, scholars have retrieved fragments of the poem.

Medieval Icelanders thus seem to have treated sex with a barnyard realism quite at odds with the idealizing romanticism of contemporary Europe. Yet in one area of behavior, sex in the sagas seems charged with a dark explosiveness. This is where hints of homosexuality come to the surface. In

Njál's Saga, Skarp-Heðin taunts Flosi by suggesting that he is "the mistress of the Svinafell Troll, who uses you as a woman every ninth night." In Gísli's Saga, Gísli's enemy Skeggi, intending to humiliate the hero, tells his carpenter to make wooden figures of Gísli and his friend Kolbjörn "and have one stand close behind the other"—an imputation of sodomy. One of the more surprising grounds for divorce in early Iceland was if a man wore effeminate clothing, or a woman manly garb. Men normally wore high-necked shirts, while women wore low-cut gowns. If a man wore a shirt open enough to expose his nipples, or a woman wore breeches, this was sufficient cause to invoke the law. The rigor of such penalties, along with the prevalence in the sagas of jeers like Skarp-Heðin's, argues that homosexuality must have been rampant in medieval Iceland and that it was regarded as shameful.

Since saga times, visitors and natives alike have been struck by the beauty of Icelandic women. Richard Burton, that connoisseur of the erotic from Arabia to Utah, waxed rhapsodic about the shades of the women's hair:

> The color ranges from carroty red to turnip yellow, from barley-sugar to the blond-cendré so expensive in the civilized markets. We find all the gradations of Parisian art here natural; the corn golden, the blonde fulvide, the incandescent (carroty), the florescent or sulphur hued, the beurre frais, the fulvastre or lion's mane, and the rubide or mahogany, Raphael's favorite tint.

Magnússon writes, "One of the compliments most often repeated by foreign visitors and relished by the natives is to the effect that Icelandic women are among the most beautiful in the world." The world traveler Jan Morris concurs: "Everybody who goes to the island is struck by the splendor of the girls." Between 1985 and 1988, the winner of the Miss Iceland contest was twice crowned Miss World and once finished third. Before 1985, feminists in Iceland had organized against the beauty contest. Their protest fizzled out after Hófi Karlsdóttir won Miss World, because Icelanders value excellence at the international level above any political stance.

The two most complex and important women in the sagas are Hallgerd in Njál's Saga and Guðrún in the Laxdaela Saga. It is significant that each is singled out as a paragon of beauty and that each has a series of husbands—Hallgerd three, Guðrún four.

Hallgerd is described as a striking child "who had grown up to be a woman of great beauty. She was very tall, which earned her the nickname Long-Legs, and her lovely hair was now so long that it could veil her whole body. She was impetuous and wilful." The attention to her hair, of course, foreshadows the climactic scene in which her husband Gunnar, besieged by his enemies, asks her to weave some strands of her hair for a bowstring.

The saga author has mixed feelings about Hallgerd. He admires her forcefulness, pride, and beauty. But on the very first page, Hallgerd's father kisses his little girl and asks his brother if she is not beautiful. The uncle hesitates, then darkly predicts: "The child is beautiful enough, and many will suffer for her beauty; but I cannot imagine how thief's eyes have come into our kin." Grown up, married into power, Hallgerd manipulates behind the scenes, causing at least three deaths. And she fulfills her uncle's intuition, ordering a slave, during a time of great famine, to steal large amounts of butter and cheese from a neighboring farmstead. It is upon discovering this deed that Gunnar slaps his wife.

There is no mistaking the saga's condemnation of Hallgerd for her refusal to save Gunnar's life by twining her hair into a bowstring. Gunnar is too proud to ask twice, but his mother has the savage last word: "You are an evil woman, and your shame will long be remembered." Nonetheless, among modern Icelandic feminists, Hallgerd has become a kind of patron saint.

Guðrún, we are unequivocally told, "was the loveliest woman in Iceland at the time, and also the most intelligent." She was "a woman of such courtliness that whatever finery other women wore, they seemed like mere trinkets beside hers. She was the shrewdest and best-spoken of all women; and she had a generous disposition."

Guðrún is married at fifteen against her will, but succeeds in tricking her husband into wearing an effeminately open shirt, and wins a divorce. Like Hallgerd, she is a master manipulator; she is also overfond of jewelry. Widowed by her second husband, she meets Kjartan at the baths and falls in love with him. The feeling is mutual, but Kjartan has his heart set on a journey abroad. When he leaves Iceland for three years, Guðrún, in a pique, marries his foster-brother Bolli instead. The passion between Guðrún and Kjartan persists, but takes a nasty turn. She manages to shame Bolli into killing his own beloved foster-brother. In turn Bolli is hunted down and killed.

The triangle among Guðrún, Kjartan, and Bolli is the single great love story in the sagas. It manifestly echoes the Germanic tale of Siegfried and Brunhild in the *Nibelungenlied*. Although Guðrún does not appear on stage until halfway through the *Laxdaela Saga*, the centrality of the doomed love affair, along with certain chivalric features, has led scholars to argue that it is the most European of the sagas—and thus, to some extent, the least purely Icelandic. But in all other respects, the saga is a solidly native work.

Guðrún marries a fourth time, only to be widowed once more, when her husband drowns at sea. In her old age, she becomes a devout Christian, the first nun in Iceland. At the end of the saga, her son visits her and asks which of her four husbands she loved the most. She answers cryptically, "I was worst to the one I loved the most." This is the most famous riddle in the sagas: for seven centuries, readers have argued over whom Guðrún meant.

Guðrún spends her last years at Helgafell ("Holy Mountain"), on the north coast of the Snaefellsnes peninsula in western Iceland. She is supposedly buried south of the mountain, just outside the yard of the church that stands there today; a fenced plot, lush with weeds, marked by a simple headstone, declares her resting place. In 1897 Collingwood gained permission from the local farmer to excavate the grave. He found "an undoubtedly ancient tomb, built of masonry," "fragments of bone and grave earth," but "no valuable relics; perhaps none should be expected in a Christian grave." (It seems shocking that this otherwise sensitive Victorian, who deplored Iceland's neglect of its early churches, should have plundered an eight hundred-year-old burial site, one of the country's most cherished locations, without a qualm. It was an age, of course, when there was little difference between professional archaeology and grave-robbing.)

Helgafell was a holy mountain before it was Christian. The Thórsnes peninsula, a small lobe of land protruding north from Snaefellsnes, is one of the two most sacred sites in Iceland, along with Thingvellir. The *Eyrbyggja Saga* tells us why.

Banished from Norway by King Harald Finehair, a powerful chieftain

named Thórólf Mostrarskegg decides to settle in Iceland. Like Ingólf Arnarson only a decade before him, Thórólf casts overboard his high-seat pillars, which are carved with the image of Thór. They drift to shore at a place he calls Thórsnes. Thórólf was a swaggering fellow: he "lived in a grand style," the saga tells us, and "was a great friend of Thór." He at once builds a magnificent temple to the god. Thórólf is deeply struck by the mountain he names Helgafell, even though it is a rather ordinary hill only 240 feet high. The saga captures Thórólf's pomposity as he consecrates his settlement:

> For this mountain Thórólf had such great reverence that no man might look at it without first having washed. Nothing was to be killed on this mountain, neither cattle nor human beings, except those cattle which left there of their own accord. That mountain he called Helgafell; and he believed that he would enter it when he died, and also all his kinsmen on the ness. At the place where Thór had come ashore, on the point of the ness projecting into the sea, he had all the courts held. And there he established the district assembly. This too was such a holy place for him that he would not allow it to be defiled in any way whatsoever, either through bloodshed or through human excrement. For this purpose a skerry [rocky island] was set aside which was called Dirtskerry.

It is this last provision that proves too much for Thórólf's neighbors. Tired of "the arrogance of the Thórsnes people," a distruntled group announces at the assembly "that they would ease themselves on the grass there as anywhere else. . . . They stated openly that they would not wear out their shoes going to the skerry for their needs." The squabble turns into an armed battle,

LEFT: HORSES FACE AWAY FROM A MARCH WIND ON SNAEFELLSNES. THE ELDBORG CRATER IS IN THE LEFT DISTANCE.

CENTER: THE "BLOODSTONE" FROM THE ALTAR OF THÓR AT THÓRSNES, LONG CONSIDERED BY LOCALS TO BE THE SITE OF HUMAN SACRIFICES.

RIGHT: THE GRAVE AT HELGAFELL OF GUÐRÚN ÓSVÍFRSDÓTTIR, "THE LOVELIEST WOMAN IN ICELAND, AND ALSO THE MOST INTELLIGENT," ACCORDING TO THE LAXDAELA SAGA.

OVERLEAF: THE AUTHOR PAUSES ON A WINTER ASCENT OF SNAEFELLSJÖKULL, THE MOUNTAIN ON WHICH THE SAGA HERO BÁRÐR EXILED HIMSELF AFTER SLAYING HIS NEPHEWS.

with men killed on both sides.

The Thórsnes-Thing was one of only two local assemblies in Iceland that predated the Althing. It is still possible to see today, on the slender tongue of land above the sea, the "bloodstone" of the pagan temple. Both Collingwood and Burton visited the place. The latter accepted on faith the saga's claim that human sacrifices had taken place there. Collingwood demurred: "Here perhaps there may have been some tradition of human sacrifices to justify the saga-man: but there is not a morsel of evidence that it was part of their system of law and religion after settling in Iceland."

In keeping with Iceland's reticence about its famous sites, no billboard nowadays urges a visit to Helgafell. The basalt mound is a ten-minute walk to the top, where there are fine views south to the chain of high mountains that form the spine of Snaefellsnes, north over the many islands of Breiðafjörður. Close at hand below stands the handsome church with Guðrún's grave. A stone-walled windbreak and a view-dial decorate the summit, but no historic plaque or sign.

Yet Helgafell retains something of its supernal charm. An old superstition holds that on your first climb of the mountain you will be granted three wishes; if you do not look back or speak a word, if the wishes are not evil, if you do not reveal them to others, and if you face east. As you walk the trail that ascends Helgafell from the west, you find yourself observing the ritual to the letter. Whether your wishes come true, only Icelandic Fate will tell.

Nearly all today's visitors to Iceland come during the summer. This was

equally true in the nineteenth century: Baring-Gould, Morris, Burton, Collingwood—and, for that matter, Auden in 1936—all fit in their journeys between June and September.

In winter Iceland is a different country—the lava fields shrouded in snow, sea ice pinching the northwest coasts, the horses shaggy in their hibernal coats, the great darkness dominating the day. Yet even during the Saga Age, in winter men traveled great distances overland, fished in the dangerous sea, and fed their livestock with hay laid up over the summer. The Vikings recognized only two seasons, winter and summer. Winter was reckoned to begin on the Saturday in October that fell between the 11th and 17th of the month. It was the occasion for one of the biggest feasts of the year—a formal welcoming of the season, with drinking of ale, eating of freshly-slaughtered cattle, and sacrifices to Frey, the god of fertility.

In the winter of 1989, this writer and his photographer-partner decided to try to climb Snaefellsjökull, Iceland's most famous mountain. We felt that an ascent in early March would give us direct inklings of the ordeals the inhabitants of this rugged country had undergone, largely beyond view of the rest of the world, through more than 1,100 subarctic winters.

At a mere 4,744 feet, Snaefellsjökull is not Iceland's loftiest summit. It stands, however, at the very tip of Snaefellsnes, at what is nearly the westernmost point of Iceland. A dormant volcano rising straight from the sea, it catches the untempered fury of the blizzards and hurricanes that roar across the Denmark Strait separating Iceland from Greenland. On a clear summer's day in Reykjavík, Snaefellsjökull stands like a white beacon in the northwest, seen across seventy-five miles of water as the sun sets behind it. For early mariners, it was a sovereign landmark.

Snaefellsjökull is the setting for Jules Verne's *Journey to the Center of the Earth*, published in 1864. Verne's German adventures stumble across some old runes that direct them to Iceland. After an arduous horse-trek to the end of the Snaefellsnes peninsula, they attack the mountain with enough gear to outfit an Everest expedition: six months' food (meat extract and biscuits, gin but no water), six pairs of boots per man, rifles and revolvers, mattocks and pickaxes, a hammer and iron spikes, and a three hundred-foot silk ladder. Even so, they reach the verge of defeat before they come upon a miraculous basalt staircase that leads them to the summit. From there, the descent to the center of the earth follows like clockwork.

At the time Verne wrote his novel, Snaefellsjökull was still unclimbed. The French author, in fact, never traveled to Iceland; for his account, which is full of apparently realistic observations of natives, architecture, Icelandic food, and the like, he relied on travelogues and on his fertile imagination.

Snaefellsjökull was attempted by British adventurers as early as 1815, at which time the locals said that no Icelander had ever been higher than the line of permanent snow, perhaps 2,000 feet below the summit. In 1859 or 1860, a good English mountaineer named Charles S. Forbes recruited a party in Ólafsvík, the town on the north side of the mountain, for an attempt in August. The locals told Forbes the ascent was impossible, and when he hired two of their number as guides, their relatives mourned them as goners. Befuddled by crevasses and a storm, Forbes renewed his efforts: "I attached the party Alpine-fashion; and leading the way, occasionally encourag[ed] my companions with brandy and snuff." Still, he failed. Some forty years later,

Collingwood was content to gaze at the mountain from Ólafsvík, "inaccessible as it is—and except by the crazy foreigner unattempted."

It is not clear who made the first ascent of Snaefellsjökull; it may have come around the turn of the century. By today's standards, the mountain is not a difficult outing, especially in summer, when climbers pave a safe route through the crevasse fields that guard the upper regions. Fittingly, the hardest part of the mountain is its summit, one of a pair of 100-foot rock towers that even in August are plastered with rime ice. Snaefellsjökull is still seldom climbed in winter, when, if the weather turns bad, it can be serious business. As experienced alpinists, Jon Krakauer and I felt we could handle the technical demands of the summit tower. Catching the right weather, however, and, in March, simply getting *to* the mountain, were separate matters.

In Reykjavík, we rented a four-wheel-drive Land Cruiser with studded tires and set out on the 12th of March. Through a long, nerve-wracking day we drove on increasingly marginal roads. Highway 54, which hugs the south coast of Snaefellsnes, was drifting steadily with fine snow blown inland by a storm over the Faxaflói. We would drive for an hour or two without seeing another car. At times we could discern the road only by peering at the skimpy line of wooden stakes marking its right shoulder; through the drifts, our wheels plowed a path as deep as a foot and a half. In the odd homestead set well back from the road, we knew farming families were battened down for winter, but we scarcely saw a person outdoors all day.

Yet the drive was breathtaking, with low sun filtering through whipped spindrift, the mountains to the north shagged with ice, flocks of birds dancing on updrafts that welled out of sinister black couloirs. The whole journey, like any other in Iceland, took us past one blank landmark after another, the name of each evoking some dark or heroic moment of the fabled past. On our left, the bay called Hvalfjörður, where the Black Death came to Iceland in 1402. Geirshólmi, the island in the bay from which Helga Jarlsdóttir swam to safety with her two young sons, escaping robbers during the Saga Age. The long plateau called Akrafjall, refuge of the eighteenth-century thief Arnes; when a party went looking for him, he infiltrated himself into the group and joined the search. A sharp tuff ridge protruding from a high peak on the right, where Grettir the Strong hid under a shelter made of homespun cloth. The farmstead of Staðastaður, set well back on the right, home of the great historian Ari the Wise, where another hero, so says the folktale, was dragged by a shaggy paw into the sea. The sharp cliff called the Knarrarklettar, over which many travelers through the ages, blinded by snowstorms, have fallen to their deaths. The plain farmhouse of Öxl, set square beside the road, where Iceland's worst mass-murderer, Axlar-Björn—no myth he—killed some eighteen passersby in the sixteenth century.

At dusk we pitched our tent a few miles southeast of Snaefellsjökull, right on the highway, so unlikely did we think it that another vehicle would come along in the night. We were wakened at 2:00 A.M. by a vicious 60-mph gale that threatened to wreck the tent. We stayed up most of the rest of the night pressing the walls with our feet and backs to keep the aluminum poles from snapping. A little before dawn, when the wind relented, we dropped off to sleep, having given up much hope for the ascent. But at dawn, the sun was out, turning the world to a dazzle of ice and sea. There was still a stiff wind in our faces, but we strapped on our skis and started up the mountain.

OVERLEAF: SPINDRIFT SWEEPS THE SOUTH COAST OF SNAEFELLSNES, WHILE A WALL OF WARM, DRY WIND (FOEHN) BUILDS OVER THE LEE SIDE OF THE MOUNTAINS.

Of all the kinds of landscape in Iceland, the sagas pay least attention to the glaciers. The great icecaps and glaciated peaks like Snaefellsjökull seem always to have been a terra incognita. Other remote and frightening places—caves, waterfalls, the depths of lakes—were the lurking grounds of monsters, trolls, and giants. The Icelandic glaciers, for the most part, were uninhabited even by spirits.

The salient exception is Snaefellsjökull, the principal scene of the little-read but fascinating *Bárðar Saga*. Few of the sagas deal more thoroughly with the supernatural. Bárðr himself, the hero, is only half human, for he is descended on his father's side from both giants and trolls. The tale abounds in trolls, elves, and dwarfs, many living in caves. One of its most chilling scenes is a wedding feast in a cave that turns into a Walpurgis Night. The unwilling human bride is bound to a chair. The trolls dine on horsemeat and human bodies: "They began to eat and tore the flesh from the bones like eagles and fighting bitches." Trolls and humans end up maiming each other in a bone-throwing contest that culminates in mass beheadings.

According to the saga, Bárðr himself is the man who named Snaefellsjökull as he saw it from the sea on an early voyage of settlement. (The Icelandic compound name prosaically enough, means "snow-mountain-glacier.") The crucial action of the saga begins innocently. Bárðr's tall, beautiful daughter Helga is roughhousing on the shore with her two male cousins. They push her onto an ice floe that drifts out to sea and carries her all the way to Greenland. There she is rescued by Eirík the Red, but it is three years before she is able to return to Iceland.

At his daughter's disappearance, Bárðr flies into a rage. He seizes his nephews about the waist and carries them up onto Snaefellsjökull, where he throws one into a crevasse, the other off a cliff, killing both. Later, in a wrestling match, he breaks his brother's leg. In remorse, Bárðr flees human society, climbing the mountain to hole up in a cave that no one can find.

Although all the trolls and giants in the *Bárðar Saga* are evil figures, Bárðr becomes one of the *landvaettr*, a benevolent guardian spirit of the mountain and, by extension, of the whole peninsula. He is never reconciled to human companionship; but at intervals through the rest of the saga, he makes shadowy appearances, always wearing a gray cloak with a walrus-hide rope for a belt, carrying a two-pronged staff with feather blades that he digs into the ice as he crosses the glacier. In this most wintry of the sagas, Bárðr rescues a man in trouble fishing at sea during a snowstorm, another man benighted during a winter traverse of the mountain, and his own son, who locked in the grotesque bone-throwing contest with the drunken trolls.

Over the centuries, belief in Bárðr took contrary forms in such local villages as Ólafsvík and Arnarstapi. On the one hand, since he still resided in his cave on the mountain, the gray-cloaked wanderer might keep an eye out for travelers in trouble. On the other, he guarded his mountain against human interlopers: it was for this reason, as much as any, that Englishmen such as Forbes were told that the ascent was impossible.

As we skied up the lower slopes of Snaefellsjökull, Jon and I gradually passed to the right of the jagged crest of Stapafell, a satellite peak whose summit, according to old tradition, is a dwelling place for elves. We must have skied near Sönghellir, where Bárðr, in his first days ashore, found a cave full of echoes that he knew were dwarf-talk. Undaunted, he made Sönghellir

FISHING BOATS LIE MOORED AT ANCHOR AT ARNARSTAPI NEAR THE TIP OF SNAEFELLSNES.

OVERLEAF: A RARE BREAK IN THE SNOWFALL REVEALS THE TWIN SUMMITS OF SNAEFELLSJÖKULL, LOOMING IN THE DISTANCE.

the meetingplace for the councils of his men. The *Road Guide* insists you can still see old inscriptions inside. In the wind and spindrift, with the day hastening by, we had no time to look for this sacred lair.

By midmorning, the summit had been swallowed in heavy cloud, and clouds were gathering over the Faxaflói. Still, there were sunbreaks dancing on the sea, and the wind was no worse than it had been. The climbing skins we had strapped under our skis gripped the mottled ice. As the cloudcap had briefly lifted, we had caught a glimpse of the summit towers, and now the memory of that sight pushed us onward.

Around noon, however, the descending cloudcap engulfed us. Just before it did, I took a compass bearing on Stapafell, now below us in the southeast. Finding the summit in a whiteout ought to be a matter of simply climbing as high as we could, but when it came time to descend, it would be easy to get lost. We stopped for a dispirited lunch in the snow, then headed on. The world was reduced to a gray tunnel of flying sleet. It would have been hard to see a crevasse even if you stepped into one. The wind picked up, still in our faces, and we grew chilled, even though we were wearing every piece of clothing we had brought.

By 2:00 P.M. we were almost ready to call it quits. We stopped to consult, and decided to give it ten more minutes' effort. The slope seemed to be getting steeper, but it was as featureless as ever. I felt close to exhaustion.

Suddenly Jon yelled, "There it is! The summit!" Out of the murk, a dim black tower loomed. We tore off our skis, put on crampons, and got out our

DURING THE ASCENT OF SNAEFELLSJÖKULL, LOWERING CLOUDCAP SWALLOWS THE SUN. AT LEFT, THE RIME-ENCRUSTED SUMMIT TOWER, ONCE CONSIDERED UNCLIMBABLE, POKES ABOVE THE STORM.

150

ice axes. The near side of the tower looked vertical, unclimbable, but we thought we could edge around to the right and find an arête of rime ice on the backside.

In 1872, as his ship sailed around the tip of Snaefellsnes, Richard Burton had stared up at the twin-towered summit and mused, "The apex has never been reached, and we at once see the reason why . . . . Alpines who love 'climbing for climb' must remember that without ropes and ladders, perhaps kites also, and very likely with them, it will be impossible to do more than has been done by their predecessors." The year before, riding at sunset along the difficult coast, with Snaefellsjökull immersed in haze at his back, William Morris had turned in his saddle, and "saw it all darker still from the wearing of the evening and my having been staring at the bright west, but above the shadowy cliffs showed now two sharp white peaks, so much brighter than the sky, so much nearer-looking than anything else, that I started almost with terror as if the world was changed suddenly."

Not with kites and ladders, but with axe-picks and crampon-points and a century's progress in alpine technique, Jon and I clawed our way to the small frost-feathered summit. The wind shrieked out of the gray nothingness. We raised our fists and cheered. Then, after a short stay, we turned to go. With the sagas in our heads, with Iceland at its wildest beneath our boots, it would not have been impossible to see Bárðr clumping along the summit ridge, prodding the glacier with his staff, ready to show us the way down.

OVERLEAF: DRIVING BECOMES NOT SO MUCH DANGEROUS AS NEARLY IMPOSSIBLE WHEN DRIFTING SNOW ERASES THE ROAD ON THE SNAEFELLSNES PENINSULA.

# SELECTED BIBLIOGRAPHY

Auden, W.H. and Louis MacNeice, *Letters from Iceland*, New York: 1969.

Baring-Gould, Sabine, *Iceland: Its Scenes and Sagas*, London: 1863.

*Bárðr Saga*, translated by Jón Skaptason and Philip Pulsiano, New York: 1984.

Bárðarson, Hjálmar, *Iceland: A Portrait of Its Land and People*, Reykjavík: 1982.

Brøndsted, Johannes, *The Vikings*, London: 1960.

Burton, Richard F., *Ultima Thule; Or, A Summer in Iceland*, London: 1875.

Byock, Jesse L., *Medieval Iceland: Society, Sagas, and Power*, Berkeley: 1988.

Carwardine, Mark, *Iceland: Nature's Meeting Place*, Reykjavík: 1986.

Collingwood, W.G. and Jon Stefansson, *A Pilgrimage to the Saga-Steads of Iceland*, Ulverston: 1899.

*Egil's Saga*, translated by Hermann Pálsson and Paul Edwards, London: 1976.

*The Elder Edda*, translated by Paul B. Taylor and W.H. Auden, New York: 1969.

*Eyrbyggja Saga*, translated by Paul Schach, Lincoln, Nebraska: 1959.

Forbes, Charles S., *Iceland: Its Volcanos, Geysers and Glaciers*, London: 1860.

*Grettir's Saga*, translated by Denton Fox and Hermann Pálsson, Toronto: 1974.

*Hrafnkel's Saga and Other Stories*, translated by Hermann Pálsson, London: 1971.

Ker, W.P., *Epic and Romance: Essays on Medieval Literature*, London: 1922.

Kristjánsson, Jónas, *Eddas and Sagas: Iceland's Medieval Literature*, Reykjavík: 1988.

*Laxdaela Saga*, translated by Magnus Magnusson and Hermann Pálsson, London: 1969.

Magnússon, Sigurður A., *The Iceland Horse*, Reykjavík: 1978.

Magnússon, Sigurður A., *Northern Sphinx: Iceland and the Icelanders from the Settlement to the Present*, London: 1977.

Marcus, G.J., *The Conquest of the North Atlantic*, New York: 1981.

Morris, William, *Icelandic Journals*, New York: 1969.

*Njál's Saga*, translated by Magnus Magnusson and Hermann Pálsson. London: 1960.

Nordal, Johannes and Valdimar Kristinsson, *Iceland 874-1974*, Reykjavík: 1975.

*The Saga of Gísli*, translated by George Johnston, London: 1963.

Steindórsson, Steindór, *Iceland Road Guide*, Reykjavík: 1981.

Verne, Jules, *Journey to the Centre of the Earth*, London: 1965.

# INDEX